ROSI MILAGROS

by

José Luis Hinojosa, MD

Also by José Luis Hinojosa, MD

NOVELS

The Tonic
Master and Disciple

PLAYS

Exam Room 2
Chameleon

NONFICTION

The Language of Winners!
¡El Lenguaje de los Triunfadores!
Report Card on Rape
Magnets for Health
Tae Kwon Do for Everyone
Frozen in Time
The HELP Secret

SCREENPLAYS

Campeón (co-author)

Cast of Characters

DON CASIMIRO PANIAGUA, a wealthy ranch owner

SIMÓN FERNÁNDEZ, a night watchman

BETHZABÉ FERNÁNDEZ, his wife

LICHA, their eldest daughter

SIMONCITO, their eldest son

ROSI, their seventh, and last, child

LUPITO, one of their sons, a few years older than ROSI

HOMERO, a friend of LUPITO

CHON TORRES, Bethzabé's cousin

DOLORES TORRES, his wife

DR. RAMÓN, a family doctor

ZACARÍAS, a curandero leader

The Fernández' three other **CHILDREN**

CHONITO, the Torres' eldest son

MARIO, the Torres' other son

Other **ADULTS** and their **CHILDREN**

Action

The action takes place in and around the hacienda and ranch of Don Casimiro Paniagua, on the outskirts of Monterrey, Mexico. Within the hacienda grounds, there are several small homes which house employees and their families.

Time

The play starts in the summer of 1924.

Act I

SCENE 1

SETTING: *A small, but orderly kitchen in the home of SIMÓN FERNÁNDEZ. The walls are made of adobe and the floor is dirt. There are wooden beams on the ceiling. In the back wall there is a run-down doorway with multiple pencil-marks at pre-school kid height, extending to either side and down to the floor. In the wall to the right is a window with the curtains drawn shut. One side of the curtain is conspicuously shorter than the other, as if a piece was cut off. In the opposite wall, to the left, is a basic, white, single-door refrigerator. In the foreground stands a small, square, tin table with a Coca-Cola logo in the middle. The logo is partially covered by a fresh kilogram of corn tortillas, wrapped in butcher paper. Next to the tortillas sit the salt and pepper shakers. The table legs stand on two flat strips of wood. Four foldable chairs, also tin, are in place around the table. Over the table, a single light bulb hangs from an electrical cord attached to a beam on the ceiling. The refrigerator cord connects to an outlet on the base of the bulb. All around the kitchen there are numerous plaster figures of colorful roosters, standing proud.*

It is pitch black, sometime after midnight. SIMONCITO, half-asleep, is pushed through the doorway by a tip-toeing LICHA, who is carrying a kerosene lamp in hand. Both are barefooted. LICHA, a rotund 13 year old girl dressed in an over-sized T-shirt, looks around and rushes to the table. She puts the lamp down, swiftly opens the package of tortillas, takes one from the middle of the pack, sprinkles salt on it, and eats. SIMONCITO, a few years younger, is thin and is dressed only in boxer shorts. He rubs his eyes and walks toward her.

SIMONCITO. *¿Por qué yo, Licha? Dime, ¿yo qué te hice?*

LICHA. *Shhh, ¡cáyate!* You're gonna wake up the whole neighborhood.

SIMONCITO. *(Frustrated)* Ahhh... There is no neighborhood here. *(Goes to window and lifts curtains.) Mira -- no se ve nada.* There's nothing out there.

LICHA. Sure there is. What about *Tio Chon y Tia Dolores* house, eh?

SIMONCITO. But they're not a <u>neighborhood</u>. They're family. *(Hears a ruffle.)* What was that?

LICHA. Nothing. Didn't you just say...? *(Mimics him.)* ...there's nothing out there? *No se ve nada.*

SIMONCITO. No, honestly. I did hear something.

LICHA. Simoncito, stop it! *Me quieres asustar, ¿verdad?*

SIMONCITO. No, I don't want to scare you, Licha. *(Lets go of curtain.)* You're right. It was probably one of the cats outside.

LICHA. ...or one of the *chivos*. You know how they're always getting into things.

SIMONCITO. Yeah, and they're always <u>eating</u> stuff.

LICHA. *(Remembers she's hungry, prepares another tortilla, and continues eating.)* Anyway, what I'm trying to tell you is that we don't want *mamá*, or even worse, *papá*, to see what we're up to.

SIMONCITO. We? Licha, we? <u>You're</u> the one that's always hungry! Don't blame me.

LICHA. Well, I can't help it. Every time *mamá* is about to have another one... *(Makes hand gestures showing a big belly. Takes a bite of the tortilla.)* ... *tú sabes, me da mucha hambre.* So, I told you, I can't help it. And besides, you're the oldest of the boys, so you <u>have</u> to protect me.

SIMONCITO. *(Louder)* Why am I always the one?

LICHA. Shhh! *(Looks around.)* It's not your fault that you're the oldest boy, Simoncito. And it's not my fault that I'm the oldest girl. I just wish they'd stop it already!

SIMONCITO. *¿Qué dices?* What are you mumbling about?

LICHA. I'm not mumbling! I'm just saying that when that new baby is born... *(Beat)* I wish I could grab it by the ankles, swing it around a couple of times, and then smash it into... *(Points to a wall.)* ...into that wall there. You see?

SIMONCITO. There you go again with that story. It's not funny anymore, Licha.

LICHA. It's not supposed to be funny, Simoncito. It's supposed to be... well, the truth. *(Beats her chest.)* *Es lo que siento adentro, hermanito.*

SIMONCITO. *(Yawns)* I'm gonna go to bed. *(Turns and starts to walk away.)*

LICHA. *(Points at him with the tortilla.)* Don't you dare!

SIMONCITO. *(Stops and pleads.)* ¡Ay Licha! *Por favor, déjame dormir.* You eat and I go to bed, *¿Sí?*

LICHA. *Simoncito, -cito, mi hermanito...* (Grabs him around the shoulders.) You know I'm scared of the dark, right? *(SIMONCITO nods.)* And you... well, you're not. You're brave! *Eres... eres un hombrecito fuerte y valiente. (Grabs his biceps.)* And so, you need to protect me, okay?

SIMONCITO. *(Sniffs into the air.)* That's strange. Smells like something's burning.

LICHA. Nothing's burning. You're probably walking in your sleep, and you're still dreaming.

SIMONCITO. No, I <u>want</u> to be dreaming, but I'm here in the kitchen with my hungry sister. *(Turns and sees smoke from behind the window.)* *¡Mira, Licha! ¡Humo!*

LICHA. *(Sees the smoke, panics, and begins to run around, screaming.)* *¡Ay mamacita! ¡Ay mamacita!* Oh, my God! *Te juro Diosito, ya no como de noche. Mira...* *(Throws the tortilla.)* *... ya se me quitó el hambre.* I'm not hungry anymore. *(Sees the smoke grow in size.)* *¡Fuego! ¡Fuego!*

(LICHA does the sign of the cross several times. SIMONCITO exits running.)

ACT I

SCENE 2

(In runs SIMÓN FERNÁNDEZ, 47 years old and head of the household. He's a handsome man with a full set of black hair and early graying on the sides. He has a thin moustache over his upper lip. SIMON quickly surveys the situation. LICHA runs to him and seeks refuge in his arms. He holds her.)

SIMÓN. Are you alright, *¿mi'ja?*

LICHA. *Ay papi, yo no fui. Te juro que yo no fui.* I swear by *La Virgen de Guadalupe*, it wasn't me.

SIMÓN. *(Looks at the tortilla on the floor, then looks at her.)* I believe you, my scared little pigeon. I believe you.

LICHA. *(Surprised)* You do?

SIMÓN. Yes. *(Firm)* What was Simoncito doing up at this hour, eh?

LICHA. Simoncito was up? He wasn't with me.

SIMÓN. Oh, really?

LICHA. *Te juro por la virgencita, papi. Ella es mi testigo. (Does the sign of the cross.)*

SIMÓN. *(Beat)* Very well. But listen to me -- right now, you must be strong. Can you do that for me? *¿Te haces fuerte, mi'ja?*

LICHA. *(Fights back tears and nods.) Sí, papi.*

SIMÓN. Go to your mother and help her get your brothers and sisters outside. *¡Todos afuera!*

¡Pronto! (LICHA exits running. SIMÓN yells after her.) ...and careful with *la bebita, ¡Rosi!*

ACT I

SCENE 3

SETTING: *Moments Later*
Outside, in front of the burning house. BETHZABÉ FERNÁNDEZ, 42 years old and pregnant at full term, sits under a tree on stage left. She holds a toddler in her arms and glows with motherhood. Next to her is LICHA, who rocks a 13 month-old baby to sleep. SIMONCITO holds a younger sibling. SIMON exits the house, stage right, carrying two small children to BETHZABÉ'S station under the tree.

SIMÓN. These are the last of them. *Tanto güerco. No sé qué vamos a hacer con tanto güerco.*

BETHZABÉ. You can start by doing a head count, Simón. Can you, please?

SIMÓN. *Está bien, está bien. Un, dos, tres, ... seis.* That's six -- six children with their mother. All accounted for.

BETHZABÉ. *(Corrects him.)* Six and a half. *(Places her hand on her belly.)* Don't forget our little Rosi, now.

SIMÓN. That's right. Six and a half -- soon to be number seven. I do hope she's the lucky one, *mi vieja.* 'Cause right about now... *(Looks at the final remains of the burnt house.)* ... we really need some good luck. *(Shakes his head.)* And on my night off, too.

BETHZABÉ. *(Rubs her belly.)* Ay Simón. Remember what my mother said before she passed on? *(Does the sign of the cross.) Dios la tenga en La Gloria. (Mimics her mother's voice.)* "La *número siete, Bethzabé. Esa niña será tu milagrito del cielo. La número siete. Protéjela --* protect her because there's a lot of evil forces that fear her energy. *Le temen a su don. Algo como lo que* ella tiene... eso es algo muy especial. Escúchame, hija mia. Listen to what your mother tells you."

SIMÓN. I remember, *mujer. Yo me acuerdo.* That's when she gave you a red rose and you decided to name the child *Rosalinda.* 'Beautiful Rose.'

BETHZABÉ. *(Does baby talk.) Sí, Rosalindita chiquita. Mi bebita. (Clears her throat.)* But we can call her Rosi, for short. And you know something, Simón?

SIMÓN. What?

BETHZABÉ. Mother was never wrong. Never.

SIMÓN. I know. She was a healer. A bonafide *curandera.*

BETHZABÉ. And not just any healer, *viejo.* She was the best soothsayer in Northern *Méjico. Era la mejor curandera y consejera de la región.*

SIMÓN. It's funny, but I do miss my *suegra.* I never thought *suegras* were supposed to be... special.

BETHZABÉ. Only the best, *mi querido esposo.* Only the best. *(SIMON grimaces and touches his back.) ¿Qué es?* What's wrong?

SIMÓN. It's nothing. *(Grimaces again.)*

BETHZABÉ. *¿Cómo que nada?* I can see, Simón. I'm not blind.

SIMÓN. You're right. *(Gathers strength.)* It was a beam from the ceiling. It was full of angry flames. *Parecía un infierno. Iva derechito a uno de los niños.* It was gonna fall right on little Lupito.

BETHZABÉ. *(Covers her mouth.) ¡Dios mio!*

SIMÓN. *No pensé... Y me tiré.* I just flew. I never knew I could move that fast, *mi vieja. (Grabs at his back, in pain.)*

BETHZABÉ. *¡Ay Dios! ¿Y luego?*

SIMÓN. I was pinned for a few seconds, I guess. But it seemed like forever. *(Struggles to remain standing.)*

BETHZABÉ. *¿Y el niño? ¿Y Lupito?*

SIMÓN. He's okay. *Ese güerco está bien fuerte.* He's as strong as an ox. Me, on the other hand, *siento un ardor bien feo.* I'm burning alive, *vieja!* I'm... burning... alive.

(His eyes roll back and he collapses next to BETHZABÉ. His arm lands on her pregnant belly, almost as if protecting the unborn child. LICHA rushes to them and removes his arm. BETHZABÉ screams and several of the children cry.)

Act I

SCENE 4

(CHON TORRES, 44 years old and cousin to BETHZABÉ, runs to the tree and toward the FERNÁNDEZ'. He looks older than his stated age and his hair is almost completely gray. He is followed by CHONITO and MARIO, his two sons, who are in their twenties. CHON and MARIO are wearing shorts, a T-shirt, and sandals. CHONITO is dressed in a shirt, blue jeans, and boots.)

CHON. *¿Qué ha pasado aquí? ¡Dios mio!* Are you alright, cousin? *(Hugs her.)*

BETHZABÉ. *(Still crying.) ¡Primo!* Yo estoy bien, pero Simón... no sé.

CHON. *A ver... (Slowly uncovers SIMÓN's back.)*

BETHZABÉ. *¡Cuidado Chon!* Careful! Simón has been burned.

CHON. *(Sees the burn.) ¡Hijo de su...!* Bethzabé, it's a bad one. I think the doctor needs to see him. *(Others present also take a look and go back in disgust, except for LICHA, who wants to help.)*

LICHA. *Mamá,* I can get some *hojas de maguey* and some water, and take care of *papi* until the doctor gets here.

BETHZABÉ. *Sí, mi'ja.* But first you must notify Don Paniagua. *Pídele que le hable al doctor.* Hurry... your father's life is in danger!

(LICHA hands baby to SIMONCITO and turns to exit.)

CHON. Wait, Licha!

LICHA. *(Stops.)* Huh? *¿Qué pasa?*

CHON. *(To BETHZABÉ.)* We don't want to bother *el Jefe* at this hour, do we? *(Turns to MARIO.)* Mario! Mario, you go fetch the doctor. *(Signals him to go. MARIO exits.)* And *Licha, tú traes el maguey.*

(LICHA looks at BETHZABÉ for approval, gets it, and exits running.)

BETHZABÉ. *(Checks out CHONITO.)* Chonito, since you're already fully dressed... *(Beat)* Wait a minute. Why are you dressed, Chonito? Everyone else is in their sleep clothes. *Mira mis güercos, todos en calzón!*

CHONITO. *(Nervous)* *Ay tia, como será usted. Yo andaba dando la vuelta porque no podía dormir.* I couldn't go in my *calzones* now, could I? I was taking a walk. You know, *tia,* I suffer from... what do they call it? In-som-nia?

BETHZABÉ. *¿Desde cuando tienes insomnia, muchacho?* I didn't know you had a sleeping disorder, Chonito. So young... *(Beat)* Listen, do me a big favor... *¿puedes?*

CHONITO. Sure. What do you need, *tia?*

BETHZABÉ. There are three roosters in the pen. Bring me the red one right now! *¡Rápido, traéme al colorado!*

CHONITO. But... but the rooster pen may have burned down too.

CHON. It didn't burn down, Chonito. Trust me. Now, do what your *tia* says and go, *mi'jo!*

(CHONITO runs.)

BETHZABÉ. *Gracias, primo.* *(Surprised)* How did you [know about the rooster pen]...? Never mind.

CHON. *(Fidgets)* Ahhh... tell me, what's a rooster gotta do with any of this?

BETHZABÉ. I must sacrifice it, Chon. *(Looks at the fallen SIMÓN.)* And there's no time to lose.

CHON. You're doing <u>what</u> to the rooster? *¿Qué haces con ese pobre gallo?*

BETHZABÉ. If I want to save Simón's life, I must kill something...

CHON. You must <u>kill</u> something, *prima?*

BETHZABÉ. Chon, listen to me and listen good. *(Points a finger at him.)* Death walks among us tonight, and I'm not about to let it take my husband! *¡No, señor!* Not tonight!

CHON. *(Stunned)* I... but a rooster?

BETHZABÉ. That dead rooster will be my Simón's salvation! Now, please, don't slow me down, Chon. I'm trying to keep my husband alive! *Si no ayudas, no estorbes. ¡Esto es caso de vida y muerte! (Gets a sudden pain in her belly.)*

SIMONCITO. The baby! The baby's coming!

Act I

SCENE 5

(LICHA returns with the maguey and a bucket of water. She wets the maguey and applies it on SIMON'S back. He writhes in pain.)

LICHA. *¡Mira, mamá! Papi* is still alive! *¡Está vivo!*

BETHZABÉ. *(Regains her composure.) ¡Gracias a Dios!* Thank you, Lord!

(CHONITO returns with a red rooster in hand. BETHZABÉ quickly grabs it from him. She holds it by the head and swings it overhead three times, suddenly twisting it on the last turn, thus killing the rooster.)

BETHZABÉ. *¡A ver, Licha! Traéme esa tina.* Bring me that bucket, now!

(LICHA brings the bucket. With a sharp, pulling motion, BETHZABÉ decapitates the rooster and drains its blood into the bucket. CHONITO vomits to one side.)

LICHA. *Simoncito, ¡cuida al primo!* Take care of Chonito!

SIMONCITO. *(Walks toward CHONITO.) ¿Y yo por qué?* It's always me. *¡El tan grandote y tirando todas las migas!* Always me.

BETHZABÉ. Simoncito, enough! *Licha, moja el maguey y pónselo a tu padre.* Wet the maguey and put it on your father's wounds... *(Waves to SIMONCITO.)* ... And leave your cousin alone. He has in-som-nia.

(LICHA wets the maguey with the blood and applies it on SIMÓN. He doesn't writhe this time.)

LICHA. *¡Mamá! ¡Mamá! ¡Ya no le duele tanto!* Papi's pain is getting better!

CHON. *¡No puede ser!* It shouldn't be happening like this!

BETHZABE. *¡Sí puede ser, Chon! Esta chingada muerte no se lleva a mi Simón.* Not tonight, Grim Reaper, not tonight.

(She lies back, holding her belly in pain. BETHZABÉ screams as lights fade to black.)

Act I

SCENE 6

SETTING: *The Next Morning*
A large guest room in the hacienda of DON CASIMIRO PANIAGUA. The walls are brick interspersed with slabs of vertical wood, varnished to a shiny polish. The floor is pine green Spanish tile. In the back wall there is a dresser with two mirrors and a solid sheet of rustic-looking, green marble top. Next to the dresser is a double door, which leads to the living room. In the wall to the left is a king-sized bed. The trophy head of an elephant is displayed over the head of the bed. There is a zebra rug at the foot of the bed.

BETHZABÉ is half-way between wakefulness and sleep. She lays in the bed, holding in her arms a crying newborn baby girl, ROSI. DON CASIMIRO and DR. RAMÓN are present in the room. DON CASIMIRO is a thin and artificially-handsome bachelor in his late 50s. Rumor has it that the finest Plastic Surgeons in Mexico have worked on several aspects of his anatomy. He's freshly showered and is wearing a red, silk robe with matching silk scarf, plus soft, leather sandals. He wears bifocals and is holding a pipe in his mouth, but chooses not to smoke it out of respect for his new guests. DR. RAMÓN is 61 years old, of medium weight and height, and exhibits advanced male-pattern baldness. He is wearing a white shirt and blue tie, which is tucked into his shirt. A stethoscope hangs around his neck.
His coat rests on top of the dresser.

DON CASIMIRO. What a pleasant surprise this morning, Doctor! *Nos encontramos con una nueva criaturita.* My humble *hacienda* welcomes this new baby with open arms! *(Stretches out his arms.)*

DR. RAMÓN. *(Dries his hands on a towel.)* You're a very generous man, Don Casimiro, and I'm sure the Fernández' are grateful for your hospitality.

(Glances at BETHZABÉ and ROSI, who are both asleep.) I'm... sure... they'll let you know when they wake up.

DON CASIMIRO. *(Laughs)* It's funny how most women who come to visit end up in one of my beds... and they <u>all</u> fall asleep! *(Laughs louder.)*

DR. RAMÓN. *(Courteous laugh.)* Anyway, Don Casimiro, I wanted to ask you about the other patient. *El otro pacientito...* I understand he's one of your workers?

DON CASIMIRO. *Sí, se llama Simón. (Does a funny voice.) Simón, ese. (Laughs)* There I go again. I made another joke!

DR. RAMÓN. Please, Don Casimiro, this is no laughing matter. *Esto es algo muy serio.*

DON CASIMIRO. I'm sorry, I'm sorry. I guess I got caught up in all the excitement. Why, with my night watchman's house burning down, and his near-death experience...

DR. RAMÓN. So Mr. Fernández is your night watchman?

DON CASIMIRO. Huh? Oh, yes, that is correct. *(Returns to his story.)* And to top it all off, Doctor, a baby is born right here, in <u>my</u> hacienda! *Esto es buen material para una novela o una obra de teatro. ¿No cree usted?*

DR. RAMÓN. Yes, indeed. *(Beat)* Don Casimiro, a lot of things have transpired since last night. And that's what I'd like to talk to you about... about the events that occurred here last night. *¿Qué pasó, realmente, anoche?*

DON CASIMIRO. My dear Doctor, you're starting to sound like a police officer. *Aparte de doctor, ¿es usted policía también?*

DR. RAMÓN. No, Don Casimiro, and I don't claim to be. The only profession I've ever known is this one. *(Lifts his stethoscope.)* And, sometimes, in my chosen profession, there are certain events that fall right on the edge.

DON CASIMIRO. On the edge of what, Doctor?

DR. RAMÓN. *Aunque usted no lo crea, mi querido Don Casimiro,* there's a fine line between medicine and the law. And it is my duty to report anything I feel may put a patient in physical and/or emotional danger. My patients' interests come first. *Usted me entiende.*

DON CASIMIRO. Of course, Doctor, of course. *(Beat)* It does sound serious.

DR. RAMÓN. I can assure you, it is very serious.

DON CASIMIRO. Very well... as far as I'm concerned, you know what I know. A couple of the Fernández kids were in the kitchen, goofing around with the electrical circuitry, and they basically burned the house down.

DR. RAMÓN. That's exactly what troubles me. It just sounds so... convenient.

DON CASIMIRO. Convenient, for whom, Mr. Sherlock Holmes?

DR. RAMÓN. That's precisely what I'm asking. Who stands to benefit from such a catastrophe, Don Casimiro?

DON CASIMIRO. Doctor Ramón, are you suggesting arson? Here, in my *hacienda?* ¡Nunca! Never!

DR. RAMÓN. Please, don't honor your name so quickly, *Don Casimiro.* We must open our eyes to the different possibilities. This particular case lends itself to suspicion.

DON CASIMIRO. *(Adjusts his glasses.)* Okay, show me so I can see.

DR. RAMÓN. Fine, I'll try my best. As you know, Mrs. Bethzabé Fernández has been my patient for many years. In fact, I have now delivered all but one of her children... and that was because little Lupito came early and I was away, in the city. Anyway, during the course of this pregnancy, Mrs. Fernández had some quite interesting concerns.

DON CASIMIRO. And just what kinds of concerns are you talking about? You know, these concerns... concern me, doctor.

DR. RAMÓN. Don Casimiro, before I go on, I ask that what I'm about to reveal must not leave this room. *Lo dicho aquí, se queda aquí.* You understand... I must adhere to the strictest confidentiality regarding my patients.

DON CASIMIRO. *Yo entiendo, Doctor. Mi pecho es una bodega de los secretos entre usted y yo. (Crosses his arms on his chest.)*

DR. RAMÓN. Very well. I shall continue. *(Paces)*One time, Mrs. Fernández came to see me regarding labor pains. She actually did had some contractions, but this was early in the pregnancy and, of course, she wasn't supposed to be in labor back then. I believe her false labor was a result of her preoccupation with a belief that someone was trying to take away her husband's job. She'd say, *"Yo sé que están tratando de quitarle el trabajo a mi Simón."*

DON CASIMIRO. Did she say who?

DR. RAMÓN. Not quite... but she alluded to some of your other workers, Don Casimiro, here in your *hacienda.*

DON CASIMIRO. *Déjeme decirle, Doctor... tengo arriba de treinta y cinco trabajadores.* I have in the neighborhood of thirty-five plus employees. It would be extremely labor-intensive, but I'm willing to help in any way I can.

DR. RAMÓN. *Gracias, Don Casimiro. Se lo agradesco.* I appreciate your help.

DON CASIMIRO. You know, his job is the most lucrative in the entire *hacienda. Es guardia de noche.*

DR. RAMÓN. *Guardia de noche, ¿eh? (Beat)* And just how much does a night watchman make in your *hacienda?*

DON CASIMIRO. *(Laughs)* I'm not falling for that one, *Doctorcito. Con que sepa que gana el doble de los demás, es suficiente.* He makes twice what everyone else makes.

DR. RAMÓN. I suppose his job is high-risk, eh?

DON CASIMIRO. You better believe it. He's like a personal bodyguard for the entire *hacienda.* We're talking big responsibilities, Doctor.*(Beat)* And with big responsibilities come big rewards. *¿No cree usted?*

DR. RAMÓN. I agree, Don Casimiro.

DON CASIMIRO. But then again, I must say that a good night's sleep is <u>priceless</u>. *Ay, lo que tiene que hacer uno para dormir como bebito...* You know, he walks around with a rifle, like one of *Pancho Villa's soldados.*

DR. RAMÓN. From what you're telling me, it doesn't surprise me.

DON CASIMIRO. I wanna make this clear, doctor... safety and security are absolutely essential around here. *No hay nada como el estar bien protegido.*

DR. RAMÓN. That's right. It would be a shame to risk losing some of your valuable... *(Looks at the elephant head on the wall.)*... trophies, Don Casimiro.

DON CASIMIRO. You're smart beyond your profession, Doctor. *(Beat)* And besides, Simón Fernández is a sharp shooter. The best I've seen. *Donde pone el ojo, pone la bala. (Makes a shooting gesture.)*

DR. RAMÓN. Would it be safe to assume that a man of your position, Don Casimiro, has a lot of enemies?

DON CASIMIRO. Yes, indeed, my dear Doctor. *Hay muchos envidiosos.*

DR. RAMÓN. So, now we're back to square one.

DON CASIMIRO. I didn't know we were keeping count.

DR. RAMÓN. We're not, but there are several things we must figure out regarding this fire. First of all, was it arson or simply an accident?

DON CASIMIRO. Okay, I'm following you.

DR. RAMÓN. If it was an accident, case closed. However, if it was arson...

DON CASIMIRO. Yes? Yes?

DR. RAMÓN. If it was arson, was it aimed at the Fernández' or was it a message for you, Don Casimiro?

DON CASIMIRO. A message? What kind of message?

(Rapid knocking is heard at the door and DR. RAMON goes to open it.)

ACT I

SCENE 7

(CHON enters, followed by DOLORES, his wife, and their sons, CHONITO and MARIO. DOLORES is wearing a very simple, yet elegant, cotton, white dress and matching sandals. CHON and his sons are dressed in a shirt, blue-jeans, boots, and sombreros. CHON removes his sombrero as he enters.)

(BETHZABÉ and ROSI wake up to the commotion.)

CHON. Message? We heard something about a message... [that needed to be delivered.]

DON CASIMIRO. *(Interrupts)* ¡Qué tal, Chon! ¡Doña Dolores! *(Bows)*

DOLORES. *Buenos dias, Don Casimiro.*

(ROSI begins to cry.)

DON CASIMIRO. Now look what you've done, Chon! *(Points to the baby.)* You've woken up the baby.

BETHZABÉ. *(Groggy) Hola... Dolores.* Chon, *¿qué hora es?* What time is it?

(CHON looks for his watch, but can't find it.)

DR. RAMÓN. It's seven-thirty, Mrs. Fernández. You slept a good two hours.

BETHZABÉ. *¡Simón! ¿Dónde está mi Simón?* I must go to him!

DR. RAMÓN. Calm down, calm down. Your husband is going to be alright.

BETHZABÉ. *¿Dónde está? El me necesita...* I know he needs me!

DON CASIMIRO. *Sí, Señora Fernández, sí.* Your husband is in the next room. And when you're feeling a bit stronger, I'll have somebody help you go to him.

DR. RAMÓN. Don Casimiro is right. You need your rest. Besides, Mr. Fernández is in good hands... your daughter, Licha, is at his bedside.

BETHZABÉ. *¡Ay, que Licha! Siempre llevando la contraria.* Always does the opposite of what she's told. She thinks she knows everything, *Doctor*.

DR. RAMÓN. Sounds like a typical teen-ager to me.

BETHZABÉ. Teen-ager yes, typical no. *(BETHZABÉ and DR. RAMÓN laugh.)* Anyway, I thank God you're here, *Doctor*, because one day my Licha will give me a heart attack. *Estoy bien segura de eso.*

DON CASIMIRO. *(Interrupts)* Mrs. Fernández, let the good Doctor go home and get some rest, eh? He was up all night. *No durmió naditita, cuidándolos a los tres.* All three of you kept him quite busy. *(Pinches baby's cheek. CHON clears his throat.)* I'm sorry... I didn't introduce you. I'm a bad host. *(Playfully slaps his hand.)* Bad host, bad host. *(Everyone laughs.)* Doctor Ramón, this is one of my workers, Chon Torres, and his wife, Doña Dolores. And these are their sons, Chonito and Mario.

DR. RAMÓN. *Mucho gusto. (Greets them all with handshakes.)*

DON CASIMIRO. Chon is my gardener, but he also runs errands for me. *(Laughs)* Is that why you thought there was a message for you, Chon?

CHON. Right, right, Don Casimiro.

DR. RAMÓN. News travels fast around here. Doesn't it, Chon?

DOLORES. *(Hastily)* Yes, yes it does!

CHON. I'm not sure I understand you, *Doctor*. We came because we were told there was a message that needed to be delivered.

DR. RAMÓN. No, I think you misunderstood. What <u>needed</u> to be delivered was not a message, but a baby!

CHON. *(Sees ROSI.) La bebita, ROSI. ¡Al fin!* Finally! *(Waves at his family to gather around the bed.)*

DON CASIMIRO. Look at her, she looks just like a pretty, little rose.

DR. RAMÓN. This pretty, little rose almost didn't blossom, Don Casimiro.

DON CASIMIRO. *¿Qué dice, Doctor?*

DR. RAMÓN. I'm saying that we hadn't gotten to the specifics of the delivery yet, but I'll tell you something: This here little one is one heck of a fighter. *Esta niña pone una buena pelea.* Already, in her first few hours of life, she's survived a terrible fire and a difficult birth. Did you know that the umbilical cord was wrapped around her neck three times? Medically speaking, that's quite rare... and quite dangerous.

BETHZABÉ. *¿Se estaba ahorcando, mi bebita Rosi?*

DOLORES. *(Does the sign of the cross.) ¡Madre Santísima!*

DR. RAMÓN. *Sí, Señora Fernández, y la verdad es... ¡no sé cómo sobrevivió!* I'm stumped! I'm absolutely stumped! *(Aside)* Damned if I know how in the world this baby survived a nuchal cord times three. Those are usually the babies who don't make it.

(Grabs ROSI and talks to her.) You know something, baby? Somebody up there must really like you. *Eres un milagrito del cielo.* That's the only explanation -- the only <u>medical</u> explanation, anyway.

CHON. *Sí, un milagrito...*

DOLORES. *(Echoes) Un milagrito del cielo.*

CHON. *(Makes an announcement.)* Since there's no messages for me to deliver, I guess we're leaving. *(Looks at his family.) ¡Vamonos!*

(DOLORES hugs BETHZABE and exits after the men. Lights fade to BLACK.)

ACT I

SCENE 8

SETTING*: Six Years Later*
It is a sunny and beautiful Easter day and the hacienda grounds are full of children, playing and running around. Most of the children are in one area, hunting for Easter eggs. ROSI is away from the crowd, searching for a special egg in places where other kids have not thought of. Her hair is neatly braided and she's wearing a pink dress, adorned with red and white flowers. Her shoes are matching and her basket is quite full, as compared the other kids' baskets.

A group of children wonder where ROSI is. Amongst them are LUPITO and his friend, HOMERO, both ten years of age. They are both dressed with worn-out tennis shoes, shorts, and colored T-shirts, LUPITO's is green and HOMERO's is blue.

CHILDREN. Rosi! Rosi Milagros! Where are you?

ROSI. *¡Acá estoy! ¡Acá estoy! (Waves at them.)* I'll be right over! I'm about to find the magic egg! *(Finds the egg, jumps with joy, and starts jogging to the children.)*

LUPITO. *¡Ándale, Rosi, te estamos esperando!* We wanna play tag. *(Turns to HOMERO.) Homero, esa es mi hermanita, Rosi.* She's the fastest girl you'll ever meet. *¡Nadie corre como Rosi Milagros! (Does a traditional Mexican yell.)*

(ROSI reaches the children and shows off her magic egg. They gather around her and everyone talks at the same time.)

ROSI. *(Raises her hands.)* Quiet! Quiet everyone! *¡Silencio! (The noise subsides.)* I am happy to announce that this is none other than... *(Playfully counts with her fingers.)* ... my <u>third</u> consecutive year finding the magic egg! *¡Tres años, y no hay daños! (Raises the egg overhead. The children applaud.)*

HOMERO. I never heard of a magic egg. What's a magic egg, anyway?

(Everyone uuuh's and quiets down.)

LUPITO. *Homero, ¿qué tienes?* What kind of question is that? *(Turns to everyone.) ¡No sé quien es!* He's not with me.

(Occasional laughter.)

ROSI. *(Approaches HOMERO.)* What? You haven't heard of the magic egg?

HOMERO. No.

ROSI. *¿De dónde eres?*

HOMERO. Why?

ROSI. *¿Por qué?(Beat) Porque quiero saber, para no ir.* I wanna know... *(Gives HOMERO a light push on the shoulder.)* ... so I won't ever go there!

(Everyone laughs.)

LUPITO. C'mon, guys! Don't be like that. *No sean gachos.* Homero is new to this area. They probably don't have Easter where he comes from. *(Turns to HOMERO.)* Do you?

HOMERO. *Pos, ¡claro!* Of course we do!

LUPITO. *(Turns to everyone.)* See? What did I tell you? *Él sabe del huevo mágico.*

ROSI. No, he didn't say he knows about the magic egg. He said they have Easter where he comes from. *(Beat)* Where <u>do</u> you come from, anyway?

HOMERO. General Treviño, Nuevo León. It's close to here.

ROSI. How close?

HOMERO. I dunno, but my dad always tells my mom, *'Estamos a un escupitaso de Monterrey, vieja.'*

ROSI. Well, let's see, then.

HOMERO. What?

ROSI. Let's see how far you can spit. You say it's close enough to spit at. Let's see you do it.

HOMERO. *(Shyly)* Nah!

LUPITO. Just leave him alone, Rosi. He doesn't wanna spit.

ROSI. Aw, c'mon, Homero! I'll spit if you spit.

CHILDREN. *(Joining in at random.)* I wanna spit too! Hey, I'll spit! Did somebody say spit?

HOMERO. Well, alright.

(Everyone cheers.)

LUPITO. *¡No tienes qué, Homero!* You really don't have to. *(Looks around.)* Look at you guys. You're all getting your saliva ready. *(Turns to HOMERO.) Está bueno, Homero, si escupes...* If you spit... *(Beat)* ... you'll be my best friend forever!

CHILDREN. *(Chanting and clapping in rhythm.)*
¡Quiere escupir! (Clap, clap.)
¡Quiere escupir!(Clap, clap.)
¡Quiere escupir! (Clap, clap.)

(HOMERO prepares himself. He expertly brings up a glob of phlegm and holds it in his mouth. He assumes a ready stance, runs his fingers through his hair, and then he fires the glob much like a bullet coming out of a revolver. It strikes the leaves from a tree about ten yards away. Everyone uuu's and aaa's.)

(ROSI runs to the tree to verify that it is HOMERO's spit. She runs her index finger across a leaf, inspects it, and then runs back. The CHILDREN are talking.)

ROSI. *¡Silencio, todos!* Listen up! *(Raises her index finger. Everyone quiets.)* I have one thing to say and one thing only! *(Looks at her finger.)* Esto, mis estimados amiguitos, ¡no es crema! This is not cream on my finger!

(Playfully shows it to several children as if to stain them. They gross out. ROSI chases them offstage.)

Act I

SCENE 9

HOMERO. Hey, Lupito, your sister is something else. She runs pretty fast too, for a girl. What grade is she?

LUPITO. She's in first grade. *Tiene seis.*

HOMERO. Wow, *tan chiquita y ya manda a todos estos.* She's always bossing everyone around?

LUPITO. Sometimes, but she's really not bossy. She's <u>special</u> and they all like her. They wanna be like her. She's Rosi Milagros.

HOMERO. Yeah, I heard everyone calling her that. What's up with that? *¿Qué onda?*

LUPITO. My mom says she was a miracle baby.

HOMERO. What do you mean miracle?

LUPITO. Well, Rosi was never supposed to be born.

HOMERO. Huh?

LUPITO. Yeah, my grandma told my mom that Rosi was gonna have special powers and to be careful.

HOMERO. Careful with what?

LUPITO. With everyone who was jealous and who didn't want her around. Mainly, the bad spirits.

HOMERO. You're freaking me out, Lupito. *Creo que me estoy mareando.* I think I'm gonna pass out. *(Sits)*

LUPITO. *(Also sits.)* Anyway, *mi abuela era curandera.* She was a healer. And she gave my mom many recipes to keep Rosi safe. Oh, and get ahold of this -- all this was happening <u>before</u> my little sister was born! *(Beat)* Are you listening? *(HOMERO nods.)* So, as I was saying... *(Tries to remember.)* What was I saying?

HOMERO. Something about food.

LUPITO. Food? I didn't say anything about food! Homero, are you hungry?

HOMERO. No, but you said "recipe." *Receta.*

LUPITO. *¡Ay, Dios mio!* I say recipe, but not like a food recipe, like a *curandera* recipe! It's similar to a recipe from a doctor.

HOMERO. Okay, okay. I'm sorry. I was still dizzy, okay?

LUPITO. *Bueno, te la perdono no'más porque ya eres mi mejor amigo. (Taps HOMERO on the shoulder.)* Anyway, grandma told my mom to get a bunch of roosters and put them in the house. So, we had roosters all over the place! We had them outside, we had them inside...

HOMERO. You had roosters inside? ... inside your house?

LUPITO. *Simón, ese. (Beat, then laughs.)* You're so gullible, Homero. The roosters we had inside were toy roosters. They weren't real, *hombre! ¿Qué crees? ¿Que mi familia está loca? (HOMERO is about to answer.)* Don't answer that!

HOMERO. *Yo no iva a decir nada.* I wasn't gonna say nothing.

LUPITO. *Bueno, conste. (Points at him.)* Grandma also had my mom cut off a piece of curtain, a big piece of curtain, so we could put it under her bed.

HOMERO. Why did you need a curtain? Those are for windows.

LUPITO. *¡Exactamente!*

HOMERO. What? *Y ¿entonces?*

LUPITO. *Y entonces,* my mom said that the curtain was like a window and it helped keep bad spirits away.

HOMERO. But how? Wouldn't it let spirits in, since you can <u>open</u> a window?

LUPITO. I don't know, I don't know! But you can also <u>close</u> a window, so stop asking so many questions! You should ask my older sister, Licha. She's into all that stuff, and people say she's good. She should know.

HOMERO. Okay, okay. I'll ask Licha when I meet her.

LUPITO. That's right, when you meet her. *(Smirks)* You think Rosi is bossy... *(Flicks his hand.)*

HOMERO. What? What happened? *¿Qué pasa, Lupito?*

LUPITO. No, nothing. *(Beat)* All I'm saying is... Rosi wasn't supposed to be born. And she was. And now, everyone says she's a miracle.

HOMERO. *Rosi. Rosi Milagros.*

ACT I

SCENE 10

(Enter ROSI, who pulls SIMON by the hand. They are followed by BETHZABÉ, LICHA, SIMONCITO, and the rest of the FERNÁNDEZ family, plus other ADULTS and CHILDREN from the hacienda grounds. Everyone carries with them assorted party favorites, including a piñata, which some of the adults prepare for the children.)

SIMÓN. Careful, *mi'ja.* *¡Mi espalda!*

BETHZABÉ. Remember your father's back, Rosi. It hasn't been the same ever since... *(Looks down.)*

SIMÓN. That's okay, *mi vieja.* You can say it. Go on, say 'since your father was almost killed in the fire.'

BETHZABÉ. No, that's okay. You said it good, anyway.

ROSI. *Papi, mami,* I'm sorry I caused you a lot of trouble, but I didn't know. I wasn't born yet.

LICHA. *(Mimics her.)* 'I wasn't born yet.'

SIMÓN. Licha, stop it!

LICHA. Why does she always get all the attention? The fire, the fire -- everyone forgets that I was the one...

SIMONCITO. Licha!

LICHA. ... who discovered it. *(SIMONCITO shakes his head.)* Well, it's true.

BETHZABÉ. Enough, Licha!

SIMÓN. *¡Ya estuvo bueno!* You want attention, eh? You want attention? *(Threatens to strike her.)*

SIMONCITO. *(Redirects everyone's attention.)* Lupito! Lupito, who's your friend? *Preséntalo – ¡no seas gacho!*

LUPITO. *(Drags HOMERO toward the group.)* ¡*Ándale, Homero!* Come on! *(Beat)* Everyone, I want you to meet my new best friend, Homero. Homero, this is everyone.

BETHZABÉ. *Mucho gusto, Homero.* Where are you from?

ROSI. He's from *General... General...* I know it's a general of some sort.

LUPITO. Yeah, and it's also real close that you can even spit on him

SIMÓN. Spit on him?

SIMONCITO. *(Laughs)* Who's spitting on who?

BETHZABÉ. Lupito! Look what you've started. *(Turns to HOMERO.)* So... Homero, you must be from... (Beat) Are you from General Treviño?

HOMERO. *Sí, señora.* I'm from there. *(Looks at ROSI.)* And I've heard that some people from there are pretty good at... [spitting]. Well, you know.

ROSI. Yes, we know.*(Wipes her finger. Some of the children laugh.)* Hey, everyone! *(Takes out the magic egg.)* Guess who found the magic egg?

(Children clap.)

LUPITO. Hey, Mom! Homero has never heard of the magic egg. Can you believe that?

BETHZABÉ. Why, yes, of course! Lots of people have never heard of it, but in our family, it's sort of a tradition.

LUPITO. Oh, I thought everyone knew about it. *(Turns to HOMERO.)* I guess you're off the hook, bro.

SIMONCITO. *(Puts arms around HOMERO and LUPITO.)* Mom, I'll tell him the story. You go right ahead with the *piñata. (Turns to the rest of the CHILDREN.)* And don't finish all the candy! Leave some for us! *(They EXIT as the CHILDREN clap and cheer.)*

ACT I

SCENE 11

(SIMONCITO leads HOMERO and LUPITO to a large tree -- the tree from the night when their house burned down. The tree is still quite strong. Their replacement house, still lacking in many commodities, was built about fifty yards from the old site.)

SIMONCITO. Here we go. Have a seat right over there, you two.

LUPITO. *(Runs to his spot.)* ¡Vente, Homero! ¡Siéntate aquí!

HOMERO. ¡Ay voy! *(Runs and takes his spot next to LUPITO.)* Hey, this is a great tree!

SIMONCITO. This tree, my dear Homero, has a lot of history. *Tiene historia.*

LUPITO. *(Elbows his friend.)* See, I told you.

SIMONCITO. Okay, but we'll talk about the tree some other time. Right now, let's get the magic egg story cleared up, because we don't wanna be left out of the candy from the *piñata!* Let me feel your energy, you two! *(The boys clap and cheer.)* Once upon a time...

LUPITO. Hey, Simoncito, the story doesn't start like that!

HOMERO. *(Echoes)* Yeah, it doesn't start like that!

LUPITO. Hey, how do you know?

HOMERO. I dunno. I was just, helping you.

SIMONCITO. *(Laughs)* Alright, alright. You're right, Lupito. It doesn't start like that, but I always wanted to say that! Boy, that felt great!

LUPITO. *(Looks over at the piñata.)* Come on, hurry!

HOMERO. Yeah, tell us about the egg. *¡El huevo mágico!*

SIMONCITO. The story is very simple. You know how Easter eggs are usually filled with confetti? *(The boys nod.)* Well, in many places, besides confetti, you have one or two eggs filled with...

HOMERO. With what? With what?

LUPITO. C'mon, Simoncito, tell us! *¡Dínos!*

SIMONCITO. *(Playful)* Oops, I think I forgot!

HOMERO AND LUPITO. Nooo!

SIMONCITO. *(Laughs)* I'm sorry, boys. You were just... too easy. *(Beat)*Anyway, there's usually one – yeah, just one egg -- that's filled with... *(Rubs his thumb and index finger together.)* ... dinero! Money, my friends, money!

HOMERO AND LUPITO. Uuuh!

SIMONCITO. That's right, boys! Money -- we can't live with it and we can't live without it. *(To himself.)* Or was it women? No, it was oxygen. *(Beat)* Well, it's something like that.

HOMERO. How much money is there, Simoncito? *¿Cuánto?*

SIMONCITO. Ah, good question!

LUPITO. Last year, Rosi got 10 *pesos!* *(Backhands HOMERO's shoulder.)* *¡Imagínate! ¡Un billete de diez pesos!*

HOMERO. Wow! *(Rubs his shoulder.)* That's a lot of money!

SIMONCITO. You better believe it! Hey, ten *pesos* can feed our family for two whole weeks! *¡Dos semanas!*

HOMERO AND LUPITO. Wow!

SIMONCITO. And our older sister, Licha... *(Looks at LUPITO.)* ... she eats a lot. *¿Verdad, Lupito?*

LUPITO. Right! One time, Homero, she ate <u>five</u> *tortillas* before I even finished one!

HOMERO. I also eat only one. *¡Con una lleno!*

SIMONCITO. Most of us eat only one, Homero. Trust me -- there aren't enough to go around. *(Beat)* So, that's the story of the magic egg! Any questions?

HOMERO. *(Raises his hand.)¡Sí!* *(SIMONCITO acknowledges him.)* Um, how does all the money get inside the egg?

LUPITO. Somebody puts it there, stupid! *¡No seas menso!*

HOMERO. I know that! What I mean is, <u>who</u> puts it there?

SIMONCITO. It's usually a generous person. A <u>very</u> generous person.

LUPITO. *Alguien con un corazón muy grande, Homero. Es lo que dice mamá.*

SIMONCITO. We think Don Casimiro, *el jefe,* is the one that contributes the magic egg for us, but no one has ever seen him. I guess he must be a pretty good magician himself to never get caught putting the money, eh?

LUPITO. *(Laughs)* Hey, I like that, Simoncito! A magician and his magic egg!

SIMONCITO. You're right. That is pretty good.

HOMERO. And Rosi always finds it?

LUPITO. It seems like it. She's very lucky! I think it's because *La Virgen de Guadalupe* came down once and touched her head.

SIMONCITO. Lupito! Homero doesn't wanna hear that!

HOMERO. Yes I do!

LUPITO. Yes he does! *(Leans toward HOMERO.)* Listen to this, Homero!

(SIMONCITO throws his arms up.)

HOMERO. I'm all ears. *Estoy bien... (Struggles to find the word.) ... ¡orejón!* I have big ears? *(Shrugs it off.)*

LUPITO. A long time ago, oh, about two weeks ago, Rosi told *mamá* that a beautiful woman had come to her and touched her.

HOMERO. But how did she know it was *la virgen?*

LUPITO. When *mamá* asked her, Rosi pointed to a picture of *la virgen* that we have in the house. She didn't even blink an eye. My little sister just said, 'That lady touched me.'

HOMERO. Wow!

LUPITO. And *mamá* said it was *La Virgen de Guadalupe.* She'd come to Earth to visit my little sister.

HOMERO. Because she's Rosi Milagros?

LUPITO. Yeah, that's probably it. Anyway, *la virgen* just smiled at her, then she put her hand on Rosi's head, and then she left.

HOMERO. That's it? She just touched her and left?

LUPITO. Yup.

HOMERO. She didn't say anything?

LUPITO. Nope.

HOMERO. Come on! How can she come from so far away and just smile and touch. It doesn't make any sense. *No te creo.*

SIMONCITO. Actually, it makes a lot of sense, Homero.

HOMERO. Huh?

SIMONCITO. The powers from the Heavens don't need to speak a lot of words...

HOMERO. *(Interrupts)* Right, she didn't speak <u>any</u> words!

LUPITO. Will you shut up and listen, Homero? You're speaking enough words for everyone up in Heaven. *Ya hablaste por todos los angelitos y todas las virgencitas del cielo. Así que, ¡cállate!*

SIMONCITO. *(Gets down to HOMERO's level and grabs his shoulders.)* Homero, on behalf of our family, please don't start telling this story to anyone, okay?

HOMERO. Why not? It's a pretty good story. I like it.

LUPITO. Just don't, okay?

HOMERO. But, who's it gonna hurt? This is something special. I mean, how often does *la virgen* come to visit... anybody?

SIMONCITO. Precisely! We don't want to stir things up. People are already saying that Rosi is the 'chosen one.' Whatever that means.

LUPITO. Yeah, Homero. *Mamá* doesn't want people to know because the wrong people might find out and then there's gonna be trouble.

HOMERO. What kind of trouble?

LUPITO. I dunno... shootings, killings. You know, the usual stuff.

SIMONCITO. Lupito!   Don't   exaggerate,   okay? *(Turns to HOMERO.)* Homero, nobody's gonna get shot. *¿Me entiendes?*

HOMERO. *Sí, sí entiendo. (Beat) Está bien, está bien. ¡Yo no sé nada! (Jumps back.)* Who are you people and what have you done with my friends, Lupito and Simoncito?

(A sudden cheer is heard. The piñata has been broken and the candy is flying everywhere. HOMERO and LUPITO see this and take off running, leaving SIMONCITO behind, who smiles and shakes his head as he follows. Lights fade to BLACK.)

ACT I

SCENE 12

SETTING: *Monday Morning, The Next Day*
A slightly larger kitchen in the FERNÁNDEZ replacement home. It is not a new home. Just like their previous home, the walls are still made of adobe, but there are areas covered with wooden panels. The floor is dirt and most is covered with flat boards. Just as before, there are wooden beams on the ceiling. In the back wall there is a doorway that leads to the bedrooms. In the wall to the right is a window with the curtains drawn open. The curtain is symmetrical, with neither side being shorter than the other. In the opposite wall, to the left, is a white, two-door refrigerator. Next to it is a smaller freezer, both of which are connected to an electrical cord descending from a beam on the ceiling.

In the foreground stands a round, wooden table with five wooden chairs equally spaced around it. Two tightly-tied ropes encircle one of the table legs, thus keeping it in place. On top of the table, several bottles of Coca Cola sit half empty. A large plate sits on the middle of the table, full of an assortment of sweet bread. Over the table, a double light bulb hangs from an electrical cord attached to a beam on the ceiling. One large, colorful rooster figure made of plaster stands atop the refrigerator, next to a photograph of La Virgen de Guadalupe.

It is Monday morning, the day after Easter Sunday. LICHA sits, eating sweet bread and drinking Coke. She has become a fat adult. SIMONCITO sits next to her, watching her in awe. He holds a cup of coffee in his right hand. SIMÓN and BETHZABÉ are heard talking as they enter through the doorway in the back wall.

SIMÓN. ... *¡Y eso es lo que le dije! (SIMÓN and BETHZABÉ laugh.)*

SIMONCITO. *¡Hola, padre! ¡Hola, madre! (SIMÓN acknowledges.)*

BETHZABÉ. *Buenos dias, hijo. ¿Cómo amaneciste?* How's your morning?

SIMONCITO. For now... *(Raises his cup.)* ... just fine, thank you.

BETHZABÉ. *¿Y tú, Licha? ¿Cómo amaneciste?*

LICHA. *(With food in her mouth.) ¡Con bastante hambre!* Why am I so hungry all the time? *(Pats her abdomen.)* I must have one heck of a tapeworm in here.

SIMONCITO. I also have a tapeworm. I call it <u>self-control</u>.

LICHA. There's no such thing as self-control. It's a myth.

SIMONCITO. A myth is me growing wings and flying to the moon!

LICHA. That's not a myth, that's a delusion!

SIMÓN. Alright, alright! Knock it off, both of you! Boy, if I had a *peso* for every time you two argue... *(Grabs his temples.)*

BETHZABÉ. ... we'd have enough to buy us a nice house.

LICHA. Well, this is actually a step-up from our other house, no?

SIMÓN. This is what it is... and that's it! *(Grabs his temples again.) Vieja,* get me some aspirins, will you?

BETHZABÉ. I think I'll get some myself.

LICHA. Boy, tell us something we haven't heard before!

SIMONCITO. Licha, you know exactly what you're doing to them. One day you're just gonna kill them.

LICHA. And just how am I going to <u>kill</u> my parents, Simoncito? Remember, Tio Chon and Tia Dolores couldn't do it, so what makes you think I can?

SIMONCITO. Well, Tio Chon and Tia Dolores were just plain evil. *(Beat)* Huh, the wonders of truth syrup, eh?

BETHZABÉ. Correction, *mi'jo*, the wonders of alcohol.

SIMONCITO. That's what I said, truth syrup.

SIMÓN. I can say one thing; alcohol does make you tell the truth. Children and drunks will always tell the truth. *(Beat)* ¡Pinche Chon! Damn! *(Strikes a wall.)* It was just a stroke of luck that night when your uncle got drunk and started mocking us during the fire. Me, that I helped him so much! *(Mimics CHON's voice and acts out the rescue.)* "Here's another one!" *(Goes back for another one.)* "And here's another one! What are we gonna do with so many damned kids?"

SIMONCITO. Good thing they didn't spot you, *papá.* You were... *(Makes a pinching motion.)* ... this close from going into the *cantina,* but what happened that you decided to stop?

SIMÓN. What happened was, I heard a bunch of commotion. You know, laughter and such, and you kids' names were mentioned. So, I just stood there, in the darkness.

BETHZABÉ. Your father was like the proverbial fly on the wall. *La mosca en la pared.*

LICHA. Only he was more of a wasp, and he wasn't on any wall. Someone was gonna get stung! *(Pokes SIMONCITO on the arm.)*

SIMONCITO. *¡Ay!*

SIMÓN. I'd heard everything I needed to hear. Chon had tried to burn us alive, during our sleep! Doctor Ramón was right all along. *Tenía razón.* He'd been telling us he thought it was Chon, but I didn't want to believe him. And for what? All for a stupid job!

BETHZABÉ. Hey, *viejo,* that stupid job is feeding our family.

SIMONCITO. So, who threw the first punch, *papá?*

SIMÓN. Well, I did, of course. I walked right up to him and said, 'You sonafabitch!'

LICHA. And the wasp had stung! *(Claps loudly.)* Pow!

SIMÓN. I had him good, but someone called the cops on me. Oh well, six months for me...

BETHZABÉ. And twenty years for the cousins! *Veinte años. (Beat)* Let's not talk about this anymore, shall we? It brings up many bad, bad memories. *(Wipes a tear from her cheek.)*

SIMONCITO. Like I said, they were evil. *(Beat)* Almost as evil as you, dear sister. *(Imitates a snake's tongue and strikes at LICHA.)*

LICHA. *(Explodes)* ¡Déjame! *(Slaps his hand away.)* You don't know what evil is, *hermano!* You ain't seen nothing yet! *¡Espérate y verás! (Takes out a deck of tarot cards.)* You wanna see evil? I'll show you evil. *(Cuts the deck.) Deja y te leo las cartas.* C'mon, what do you say?

BETHZABÉ. Licha, don't play around like that! *¡Ya estuvo bueno!*

SIMÓN. *(Calmly)* Put away the cards, Licha.

(LICHA huffs and puffs a bit, then stubbornly puts away the cards.)

BETHZABÉ. You know your father and I don't like you going to those <u>meetings</u>.

LICHA. They're not meetings, they're <u>gatherings</u>.

SIMONCITO. Yeah, a bunch of *curaderos* <u>gather</u> <u>around</u>... *(Does circles with his hands.)* ... and throw spells on each other. Isn't that true, sis?

SIMÓN. *(Grabs his temples.)* ¡*Vieja...!*

BETHZABÉ. I'm on it, *mi viejo.* I'm on it!

(BETHZABE goes to a cabinet, pulls out a bottle, dispenses some pills, hands two to SIMON with a glass of water, he sits and takes them. BETHZABE takes two herself, and then also sits.)

Act I

SCENE 13

(ROSI enters. She's wearing shorts and a T-shirt. Her hair is still braided, but it's losing its body. She stretches her arms as she enters.)

ROSI. What's all the noise? *¿Por qué tanto ruido? ¡No dejan dormir!*

LICHA. Well, it's about time you got up anyway!

ROSI. And a good morning to you too, Licha! That's what you get for eating at all hours of the night.

SIMONCITO. *(Follows her cue.)* I dunno, Rosi, what do you get?

ROSI. All grumpy!

(LICHA shoves her belly at ROSI.)

ROSI. Grumpy and fat!

SIMÓN. Enough already! *(Grabs his head.)* Vieja, are you sure those were aspirins?

BETHZABÉ. *Sí, mi viejo,* I'm sure. But you know something? I'm not feeling any better either. *(Beat)* I think what this family needs is some stress release.

ROSI. Oh, good! *(Claps and jumps.)* That sounds like fun!

SIMONCITO. What are you thinking of, *mamá?*

BETHZABÉ. I'm thinking of, perhaps, a vacation?

SIMÓN. *Vieja*, we've never been on a vacation our entire lives! Do you have any idea what you're saying?

BETHZABÉ. Yes, Simón, I do. And I <u>want</u> a vacation!

SIMÓN. And where are we getting the money for this <u>vacation</u>?

BETHZABÉ. Well, I've been doing some extra work and...

SIMÓN. So that's what you've been up to! All those nights, staying up late, pedaling and pedaling that sewing machine! And I thought you were just tired!

BETHZABÉ. I *am* tired, *viejo*. That's why I <u>need</u> a vacation.

SIMÓN. You were doing outside work? *(BETHZABÉ nods.)* Without consulting me?

BETHZABÉ. I couldn't consult you! I started when you were serving your time. So, I had to do something, *viejo!*

ROSI. *¡Sí, papi!* And she's really good, too! Remember my pretty dress I wore yesterday for Easter?

SIMONCITO. *Mamá* made it.

SIMÓN. Simoncito, you knew? *(SIMONCITO nods.)* Why am I the last to know? This is supposed to be <u>my</u> house! I am the father! *¿Quién manda aquí?*

BETHZABÉ. This is <u>our</u> house, *mi viejo.* And we all deserve this vacation, including you.

SIMÓN. I suppose you're right, *vieja.* I suppose you're right. *(Looks at the others.)* Everyone, pack your things! We're going on a vacation!

(Cheers. Fade to BLACK.)

ACT I

SCENE 14

SETTING: *Four Years Later*
The hacienda grounds at night. The date is February 24th, 1934, Mexican Flag Day, a national holiday. Tonight, most of the families are away from their homes, playing La Lotería, the Mexican version of Bingo.

LICHA has invited, and finally convinced, ROSI to join her in one of her gatherings, which is being held in the hacienda grounds for the first time. Nineteen curanderos, both male and female, are present. They range in age from 22 on up. ROSI, now ten years old, is wearing a black dress down to the mid-calf area, dark, flat shoes, and a black shawl over her head. LICHA, now 23 years old, is wearing a bright yellow dress with several green patches. She's also wearing many articles of jewelry around her neck, wrists, and even ankles. She is reminiscent of a gypsy woman, only much heavier. Her head is also covered with a shawl; this one is red in color.

LICHA power walks in front of ROSI. She is headed toward the leader, ZACARÍAS, a man in his forties. He is of medium height and is extremely thin, almost cachectic. ZACARÍAS mingles with several curanderos while they wait for the gathering to begin.

ROSI. Licha, Licha! Wait for me! *¡Despacio, mujer!*

LICHA. *¡Apúrate! No podemos dejar que el hermano, Zacarías, nos esté esperando.* We shouldn't keep our leader waiting!

ROSI. *No sé porque dejé que me trajeras.* Why am I here, anyway?

LICHA. You are here, little sister, so that *el hermano* can meet you. I've told him a lot about you, and he says the only way he can tell is by meeting you.

ROSI. And what if I don't want to meet him?

LICHA. You know, Rosi, kids are <u>never</u> allowed in these gatherings! Never! So, you better be glad I'm bringing you.

(They continue to walk until ZACARÍAS is in view. He waves at LICHA and goes to her.)

ZACARÍAS. *¡Hermana Licha! Qué bonito tener su energía esta noche.* It's so nice to have your energy tonight. *(Hug left, hug right.)*

LICHA. *¡Gracias, hermano! ¡Gracias! (Puts hand on ROSI's shoulder.)* As you requested, I have brought my little sister, Rosi, so you can meet her.

ZACARÍAS. *(Makes eye contact with ROSI.)* Heavens above! Spirits of the night! *(Chants)* We are honored with a special presence! *(Hug right, hug left.)* You have my condolences, sister Rosi. *Te acompaño en tus sentimientos, hermanita.*

ROSI. Thank you. Thank you very much.

ZACARÍAS. Sister Licha told me about your loss. When did your *madrecita* pass on?

ROSI. January 19th... at exactly four-o-five in the morning.

ZACARÍAS. How accurate you are, *¡hermanita!* How is it that you remember the hour? *(Looks at LICHA.)* Sister Licha did not remember.

LICHA. *(Fiddles with her jewelry.)* Well, I was tired... and it was really early in the morning... and, honestly, I'm not very good with dates and numbers. *Nunca me sé las fechas.*

ROSI. You ask, how did I remember? It's easy. That's the exact day and time when my oldest sister was born.

ZACARÍAS. I see!

ROSI. Wanna know who my oldest sister is?

ZACARÍAS. *(Hesitates, then notices LICHA looking down and away.) ¿Hermana... Licha? (ROSI and LICHA nod.)¡Hermana Licha!* How could you... [forget]?

ROSI. Some subjects she doesn't forget. *(Gestures as if eating.)*

LICHA. Okay, okay. I'm sorry I didn't remember the time of my own mother's death. But really, death is a topic I try to avoid. Too morbid, you know?

ZACARÍAS. *(Turns to the congregation and chants.) ¡Es tiempo de la junta!* Come gather all around us! *(Speaks) ¡Hermanos y hermanas!* We are gathered here tonight, at Don Casimiro Paniagua's *hacienda*, for the very first time. We thank *Hermana Licha* for allowing us to enter these humble premises. A very special cleansing awaits us. Everyone, please join me in our opening prayer!

EVERYONE. *(With synchronized fists in the air.)*
Spirits of the day, spirits of the night,
We are gathered here, to ask of you tonight,
Guide us when we're wrong, help us make it right.

Spirits of the day, spirits of the night,
Take us to the weak, we shall give them might,
Take us to the blind, we shall give them sight.

Spirits of the day, spirits of the night,
We are on your side, when you need to fight.
Fight! Fight! Fight! Fight! Fight!

(Everyone suddenly stops.)

ZACARÍAS. *¡Hermanos y hermanas! ¡Bienvenidos!* Welcome!

(Everyone cheers.)

ZACARÍAS. We are joined tonight by a very special guest. *Hermana Rosi* is here with us, on the grounds! *(Chants and stretches out his arms, palms up.)* I can feel your... energy! It is a powerful... ener-gyyy! *(Collapses)*

EVERYONE. Uuuh! *(They freeze up.)*

ROSI. *Licha, ¿qué le pasa?* What's wrong with him?

LICHA. *¡Socorro!* Help! Somebody, do something! *(Grabs ZACARIAS and shakes him.) ¡Hermano Zacarías, despierte!* Wake up! *(Runs around uncontrollably.)*

(ROSI goes to ZACARÍAS and places one hand on his chest and one over his eyes. She then takes a deep breath.)

ROSI. *¡Zacarías! ¡Escúcheme!* Listen to me! *Usted es un hombre débil.* You are a weak man and you need help. We will help you, Zacarías. We will help you. *(Blows through her mouth, removes her hands, and steps back.)*

ZACARÍAS. *(Opens his eyes and lets out a bird yell. Gets up.) ¡Esta hermanita es poderosa! ¡Escúchenme todos! Hermana Rosi* is the chosen one! Listen to me!

(EVERYONE claps and cheers.)

LICHA. *¿Qué has hecho, Rosi?* What in the world...?

ROSI. I dunno, Licha. It just felt like the thing to do. He's gonna be fine, but I think he needs to eat a little more. *(Touches LICHA's belly.)* Maybe you can help him in that department! Give him some of your *tortillas,* eh?

LICHA. Rosi! *(ROSI laughs and runs from her.)* Come back here, you little... *(Goes down on her knees and cries.)* ... ¡hermanita! Mi hermanita, Rosi. (Mumbles) Rosi Milagros.

(Cheers continue.)

Act I

SCENE 15

SETTING: *A Few Days Later*
The FERNÁNDEZ household. SIMÓN is up and around, and notices ROSI has not gotten out of bed. It is 2:00 in the afternoon. He goes to her bedroom and notices she's sweating. He touches her forehead -- she's boiling.

SIMÓN. *(Yells)* ¡Simoncito! ¡Licha! ¡Lupito! ¡Alguien, vengan para acá!

LUPITO. *(Enters running.)* ¿Qué pasa? What's wrong, *papá?*

SIMÓN. Go get Doctor Ramón, quickly! Your sister is very sick. Hurry!

(LUPITO exits running. SIMONCITO enters.)

SIMONCITO. What, Dad? *(Looks at ROSI.)* What's wrong with her?

SIMÓN. She's burning up! I was afraid of that fever that's going around, son. What's the name of it?

SIMONCITO. Typhoid... typhoid fever, I believe.

SIMÓN. Yes, I think you're right. *En la cantina,* the other day, someone was saying that this fever is gonna kill hundreds... even thousands! He mentioned some word...

SIMONCITO. Epi-de-mic?

SIMÓN. Yes! Or maybe, no... I dunno. It may be, then again, it may not be. *No sé. Ay, mi'jo,* you know I'm not the educated type.

(LICHA enters.)

LICHA. *(Looks at ROSI.) ¡Ay mamacita! ¡Se nos muere! ¡Se nos muere!* She's gonna die!

SIMÓN. Simmer down, Licha. Please try and help us out, okay? So cut out the theatrics. *(Sits on the bed. Buries his head on his hands.)* I wish your mother was here.

SIMONCITO. *(Side hugs SIMÓN.)* Yeah, me too, Dad. Me too. *(Beat)* Hey, Dad... I heard that so far, fifty-six people have died from this fever. It's mainly children, but grown-ups too.

LICHA. Oh, she has the fever?

SIMONCITO. *Sí, hermana.* Our little Rosi is gonna need a real *milagro* on this one. The *doctores* don't have any medicines for it.

SIMÓN. Look at her, *mi'jo.* She's so thin. How can somebody tolerate a big illness when they're so little?

SIMONCITO. I know, *papá,* I know. *(Looks at ROSI.)* Rosi, hang in there, *chiquita.* Hang in there. Remember, you're our little miracle, so you have to fight!

LICHA. *(Hesitant)* That's right, you fight, Rosi. *¡Tú pelea hasta la muerte! (SIMÓN and SIMONCITO look at her.)* Sorry! Bad choice of words.

(They wait quietly and motionless.)

ACT I

SCENE 16

SETTING: *Same Bedroom, But There Are Lots of Lights*
ROSI is lying in her bed, resting comfortably. Her breathing is regular and even. She is sweating profusely and awakens at the sound of her mother's voice.

BETHZABÉ. *¡Rosi, mi niña preciosa! ¡Despierta, Rosi!*

ROSI. *(Opens her eyes.) ¿Mami? ¿Eres tú, mami?* Is that you, mother?

BETHZABÉ. *Sí, mi'jita. Soy yo.*

ROSI. *(Smiles) Ay, mami,* there you are! I can see you! You're so beautiful, *mami!*

BETHZABÉ. Thank you, *mi'jita.* So are you!

ROSI. I've missed you so much! Where have you been?

BETHZABÉ. I've been resting, *mi'ja.* Resting. I was so tired, so very tired.

ROSI. That's good, *mami.* You worked very hard. That's good that you're resting.

BETHZABÉ. *¿Mi'jita?*

ROSI. *¿Sí, mami?*

BETHZABÉ. *¿Te vienes conmigo?* Do you want to come with me?

ROSI. *No te entiendo, mami.* I don't understand.

BETHZABÉ. I'm asking you, *mi'jita chula... (Extends her hand to ROSI.)* ... if you want to <u>come</u> with me?

ROSI. No, *mami,* thank you.

BETHZABÉ. You don't wish to come with me?

ROSI. I do, *mami,* but I think that if I do, that means that I'll have to die! And I don't want to die!

BETHZABÉ. But you're suffering so much, *mi'ja.*

ROSI. I know, *mami,* I know.

BETHZABÉ. So, do you change your mind?

ROSI. No, *mami.* I want to live. I'll go with you another day, but not today.

BETHZABÉ. Are you sure, my little Rosi?

ROSI. I'm sure, *mami.*

BETHZABÉ. Very well. Anything else before I leave, *mi'ja?*

ROSI. *Sí, mami.*

BETHZABÉ. What is it, my child?

ROSI. Can you get me a glass of water, *mami?* I'm very thirsty. I dunno why, I'm just very, very thirsty.

BETHZABÉ. *Ay, mi'jita.* I would love to do that, but I can't. I'm not permitted...

ROSI. Why not?

BETHZABÉ. Because now, I live in a world full of beautiful emotions and peace. There is no water here. There are no material things, *mi'ja,* only things that matter to the heart.

ROSI. Do I matter to your heart, *mami?*

BETHZABÉ. Of course you do, my child. Of course you do.

ROSI. I don't understand why you can't help me.

BETHZABÉ. Your brain is not thinking very well right now, *mi'jita.* You've lost so much water from your body. It's the high fevers, Rosi, they've caused your body's water to evaporate. Your body is asking you for water. That's why you're thirsty, *mi'ja.*

ROSI. *Ay, mami.* I know you're trying to help, but you're using big words... and I'm getting tired now...

BETHZABÉ. I love you, Rosi. You're my miracle baby and I love you! *¡Te quiero mucho, mi amor!*

(She disappears. ROSI goes back to sleep.)

Act I

SCENE 17

SETTING: ROSI's Bedroom, Three Weeks Later ROSI's bed is surrounded by her immediate family members, some crying, some holding hands, but everyone is in a solemn mood. She is now much thinner. DOCTOR RAMÓN is finishing an exam on ROSI. His face is expressionless.

DR. RAMÓN. *(Places the stethoscope around his neck.)* Well, I see no improvements. Rosi is what we call in Medicine, "status quo."

SIMÓN. What's that, Doctor? *¿Y eso qué es?*

DR. RAMÓN. "Status quo" is a fancy way of saying she's not any better, and she's not any worse either.

SIMONCITO. What do you mean, "not any worse?" Doctor, my little sister hasn't woken up for three weeks! I know I'm not a doctor, but I'd say that's really bad! *(Looks around.) ¿No creen ustedes?*

(Everyone agrees. They don't make much sound.)

DR. RAMÓN. I understand your concern, Simoncito. I didn't mean to sound that way. What I suggest at this time is, to give her a "tincture." The tincture of time.

SIMONCITO. I'm sorry, Doctor, but I don't like it when you use big words. What kind of "tincture" are you talking about? Are you making fun of us because we're poor?

DR. RAMÓN. No, Simoncito, on the contrary. Perhaps we're all tired after watching over Rosi for three weeks. She's not waking up. I don't know if she'll ever wake up! That's the honest truth. I'm sorry I can't offer you anything else.

SIMÓN. But you didn't give her any shots or anything.

DR. RAMÓN. There are no shots to give for this, *Señor Fernández.*

SIMÓN. Well, haven't they developed any sort of "treatment" for this?

DR. RAMÓN. Not in the last three weeks. No.

SIMÓN. Look at her, *Doctor!* She's a little skeleton lying on the bed. She's wasting away right before our own eyes, and we can't do a thing about it! *¿Qué nos pasa?*

DR. RAMÓN. *Señor Fernández,* I recommend prayer. Lots and lots of prayer. Prayer never hurts.

(LICHA begins to pray aloud. The others pray quietly. Everyone freezes.)

ACT I

SCENE 18

SETTING: *ROSI's Bedroom, Bright Lights Again*
ROSI is lying quietly, as before. She's no longer sweating, but she's much thinner now. Once again, her mother's voice awakens her.

BETHZABÉ. *¡Rosi, despierta mi amor! Soy tu mamá.*

ROSI. *(Opens her eyes.) ¡Hola mami! ¡Qué bueno que me vienes a visitar otra vez! ¿Sabes...? ¡Te quiero mucho!*

BETHZABÉ. *¡Yo también, mi vida, yo también!*

ROSI. *Tú siempre te vez bien bonita, mami. ¿Cómo le haces?* How do you do it to look so beautiful?

BETHZABÉ. *Mi'ja,* when love fills your heart, it's easy to appear beautiful.

ROSI. I have a lot of love in my heart, right?

BETHZABÉ. Yes, you do, *mi'ja.* You're a very loving child, Rosi.

ROSI. *¿Mami?*

BETHZABÉ. Yes, *mi'ja?*

ROSI. I'm not thirsty anymore.

BETHZABÉ. You're not?

ROSI. No. Funny how that works. Do you think my body has "evaporated" everything now?

BETHZABÉ. I don't know, Rosi. I don't know. But it hurts me so to see you suffering like this, my child. *(Extends her arm to ROSI.)* Take my hand, *mi'ja,* please!

ROSI. Why, *mami?* Why are you asking me again?

BETHZABÉ. Because you're my daughter, and you've already gone through a lifetime of pain and suffering... and you're only ten years old, *mi'jita!* Please, please take my hand and you won't have to worry about anything anymore.

ROSI. I don't know, *mami.* I think I still have some things to do before I die.

BETHZABÉ. Don't look at it as dying, Rosi. Look at it as resting. *(Turns and points.)* You see that beautiful light? *(ROSI nods.)* That's where we'll be going. It's wonderful there, *mi'ja.*

ROSI. I believe you, *mami. (Beat)* You know you're the most important person in my life, right? *(BETHZABÉ nods.)* And you know that I love you with all my heart?

BETHZABÉ. Yes, my child, yes. And <u>you</u> are the most important to me, Rosi.

ROSI. If I go with you, *mami,* can I come back and finish some of the things I need to finish?

BETHZABÉ. *(Smiles)* No, *mi'ja.* Once you go to eternal rest, there's no going back. But you won't regret it, my child. I promise you. *(Takes ROSI's hand and pulls lightly.)* Vámonos, mi'jita, vámonos ya. It's time to rest.

ROSI. *(Her body is pulled to a sitting position.)* No! No, I don't wanna die! I don't wanna die! *¡No me quiero morir!*

(Struggles with BETHZABÉ until the grip is released. ROSI falls back into the bed. BETHZABÉ disappears.)

ACT I

SCENE 19

SETTING: *ROSI's Bedroom, Same Day*
ROSI suddenly extends her right arm up in the air and she sits up in one swift motion. Everyone around the bed is flabbergasted.

LICHA. *(Does the sign of the cross.) ¡Dios mio, danos clemencia!* In the name of the father, the son, and the holy ghost!

SIMÓN. *¡Doctor, mire! ¿Qué está pasando?* What is going on?

DR. RAMÓN. *No estoy seguro, Señor Fernández.*

ROSI. *(Mumbles) ... [no] me quiero morir!*

SIMONCITO. *¿Qué dijo?* What did she say?

LICHA. *¡Se está muriendo! ¡Se está muriendo! (Runs around.)*

SIMÓN. *¡Simoncito, agarra a Licha!* Hold on to Licha, now!

(SIMONCITO starts toward LICHA when ROSI suddenly drops back into bed.)

LICHA. *(Points at ROSI.) ¡Ya se murió! ¡Ya se murió!* She's dead! She's finally dead!

(SIMONCITO tackles LICHA into the floor. Lights fade to BLACK.)

END OF ACT I

Act II

SCENE 1

(ROSI's bedroom. ROSI has just fallen back into bed, after a brief moment of sitting. LICHA has been tackled by SIMONCITO and is now struggling to get up. SIMÓN questions DOCTOR RAMÓN about ROSI's status.)

SIMON. Quickly, *Doctor!* Is Rosi okay? *¿Cómo está mi'ja?*

DR. RAMÓN. *(Examines ROSI with stethoscope, and then removes it.)* She's gonna make it! *¡Ya se salvó!*

SIMÓN. *(Clasps his hands together.)* *¡Gracias a Dios!* Thanks be to God!

(Family members hug each other and cry, except for LICHA, who gets up from the floor and shakes herself off.)

LICHA. *(Exiting)* I'm very happy she made it. Yeah, very happy.

SIMONCITO. But, how do you know, *Doctor?* All she did was sit up and then fall back again!

DR. RAMÓN. I realize that, Simoncito. But my medical experience tells me she's going to pull through.

SIMONCITO. What do you mean? *Explíquenos, por favor.* Please explain to us.

DR. RAMÓN. Well, on my exam, I noticed that her heart sounds are good, her breathing is steady, and she has also broken her fever. So, I'd say she's on her way to recovery.

SIMÓN. *(Hugs DR. RAMÓN.)* Thank you, *Doctor.* Thank you for everything! You're a God-send.

DR. RAMÓN. No, *Señor Fernández,* I believe the God-send is your little Rosi Milagros here. She's gonna do it again! She's gonna defy the odds. *Alguien allá arriba... (Points up.) ... tiene planes muy grandes para ella.*

LUPITO. *(Sees ROSI open her eyes.)* Look, everyone! She opened her eyes! *¡Ya abrió los ojos!*

(Everyone gathers around ROSI.)

SIMÓN. *¡Mi'ja, mi'ja!* Are you alright? Are you alright?

SIMONCITO. *¿Cómo te sientes, Rosi?* How do you feel?

ROSI. *(Groggy) Tengo... sed.* I'm thirsty.

SIMÓN. Quickly, Lupito, bring your sister a glass of water! *¡Un vaso de agua, pronto! (LUPITO exits. SIMÓN laughs.) ¡Un vaso de agua! (Laughter turns to crying.)*

SIMONCITO. *(Hugs SIMÓN.)* That's okay, *mi jefecito,* that's okay. Everything's gonna be alright.

(They cry.)

ROSI. *(Still supine.)* Why... why is everybody crying? *¿Qué pasó? (Tries to get up, but can't.) ¡Alguien ayúdeme! ¡Me quiero levantar!* I wanna get up!

SIMONCITO. *(Lets go of SIMÓN.)* You stay here, *papá.* I'll go help Rosi. *(Goes to ROSI.)* How you doing, little one? *(Hugs her softly.)*

ROSI. I wanna get up, Simoncito. *¿Me ayudas?*

SIMONCITO. Sure, sis. Whatever you say.

ROSI. *(Gives him her arms.) Bueno, ¡para arriba!* Lift, brother, lift!

SIMONCITO. I think it's better if I carry you,*¿no crees?*

ROSI. No, I'm strong. I just feel a little weak right now.

SIMONCITO. *(Uncovers ROSI.)* Wow! You've lost some weight, Rosi!

ROSI. *(Looks at her legs.)* No! I can't believe it! *¿Qué le pasó a mis piernas?* Where did my legs go?

SIMÓN. *(Gathers his strength and goes to ROSI.) A ver, mi'ja. ¿A ver esas piernas?* Let's take a look at those legs of yours.

ROSI. *¡A mí me gusta mucho correr!* I love to run, *papi!* How am I gonna run now?

(SIMÓN and SIMONCITO help her get to her feet. ROSI goes to a mirror.)

ROSI. *(Looks at the mirror.) ¡Aaaaay! ¡Aaaaay!* Who is that? That's not me! *¿Quién es esa en el espejo? ¡Es la muerte!* It's a skeleton! It's death! *(Sighs, and then faints into the arms of SIMÓN and SIMONCITO. They carry her back to bed.)*

Act II

SCENE 2

SETTING: *The FERNÁNDEZ Household, Fourteen Years Later*
The FERNÁNDEZ kitchen at noon, where ROSI is serving a plate of food to SIMON, who at 71, is still employed as a night watchman for an octogenarian DON CASIMIRO. The little home hasn't changed much, but some of the family members have married and moved out. Currently, only LUPITO and ROSI live here, with their father, SIMÓN.

A knock is heard.

ROSI. *(Goes to the door. Doesn't open it.)* Who is it? *¿Quién es?*

HOMERO. *(Offstage.)* It's me, Homero. I was a friend of Lupito many years ago. *¡Hace muchos años yo conocía a Lupito!*

ROSI. *(Grabs a kitchen knife, hides it behind her back, and cautiously opens the door.)* Who are you, again? *¿Quién eres?*

HOMERO. *Me llamo Homero. (Smiles)* Are you Rosi? The fastest runner in the region?

ROSI. *Sí, la misma.* Although I don't run that fast anymore. Have we met?

HOMERO. I believe so.

ROSI. When?

HOMERO. I think it was during Christmas... No, it was during Easter. Yes, that's it! It was Easter and I showed you my salivary prowess.

ROSI. You showed me your what? *(HOMERO is about to answer.)* Never mind! Don't answer that!

HOMERO. *(Laughs)* I could spit a long way! Remember? *(Mimics his spitting stance.)*

ROSI. Oh, yeah! You're the boy who had the *buenos gargajos. ¡Verdes!* They were green, too!

HOMERO. Yup, that's me. Although you didn't have to describe them in so much detail.

SIMÓN. *(A bit hard of hearing.)* What's going on? Someone needs to spit?

ROSI. No, daddy. Everything's fine. *(Turns to HOMERO.)* Come in, come in! *(They shake hands. ROSI puts the knife away and HOMERO sees it.)*

HOMERO. Was that for me?

ROSI. Well, yes and no. It was for you if you were somebody bad, and it wasn't for you if you were somebody nice. *Nunca sabes, ¿verdad?*

HOMERO. You're right; I guess you have to be careful.

ROSI. *(Looks at SIMON.)* You know, my father's hearing isn't so good anymore. I think it's all the shooting he's done all these years. Did you know he's still the night watchman here?

HOMERO. You don't say!

ROSI. Yes! And I think he averages about ten to fifteen shots per week. So many intruders trying to gain access to Don Casimiro and his money.

HOMERO. Isn't it dangerous that your father is still handling a fire arm?

ROSI. We don't use the "f" word around here. *No nos gusta.*

HOMERO. *(Confused)* The "f" word?

ROSI. Yes – "fire."

HOMERO. Oh, sorry.

ROSI. That's alright. *(Beat)* Anyway, you wanna know what? If it's dangerous for my dad to handle weapons? Are you kidding me?

HOMERO. No, I'm totally serious.

ROSI. To this day, he can <u>still</u> put the bullet where he wants it! Like Don Casimiro always says, *'Donde pone el ojo, pone la bala.'*

HOMERO. Yes, I've heard that about your father. *(Beat)* Rosi, is Lupito around?

ROSI. No, sorry. He's working right now, but he'll be back after sunset. Wanna come back then?

HOMERO. Well, I guess...

ROSI. Is it something important?

HOMERO. No, I just wanted to ask him something. But I guess it can wait.

SIMÓN. *¿Qué dicen? ¿Quién es buey?* Who's an ox?

ROSI. No one, daddy. No one. *(Smiles)* Never a dull moment around here.

HOMERO. If you say.

ROSI. Wait a minute! *(Concentrates as if going over something in her head.)*

HOMERO. What? What is it?

ROSI. I just saw something!

HOMERO. *(Looks around.)* Where? Did I miss it?

ROSI. *(Smiles and shakes her head.)* I'm sorry. I "see" things sometimes. Nothing bad, just little bits and pieces of...

HOMERO. ... of the future?

ROSI. Yes. How did you know?

HOMERO. When we first met, I never forgot how everyone said you were a miracle. And then, years later, there were rumors that you had these... powers.

ROSI. What kind of powers?

HOMERO. I dunno. People would say you had a gift. That you were hand-selected to do some sort of work or something.

ROSI. So, if I was hand-selected, I should know why you're here, right?

HOMERO. Right...

ROSI. But I don't. So why are you here?

HOMERO. Honestly?

ROSI. Yes.

HOMERO. Because I had a psychic tell me to come and talk to you.

ROSI. Oh, really? What else... did this psychic tell you?

HOMERO. *(Hesitant)* Ah... crazy stuff, really.

ROSI. Crazy? How crazy?

HOMERO. *(Laughing)* Get a load of this... She said someone close to you was a very bad person and that this person was going on a very long trip.

ROSI. *(Laughs, then suddenly stops.)* She's right.

HOMERO. *(Suddenly stops laughing too.)* What?

ROSI. Yup. My sister Licha eloped with Zacarías, a curandero she was totally ga-ga over. We have no idea where they took off to. (Beat) So, Homero, do you believe in psychics?

HOMERO. I thought I didn't. Now, I'm not sure.

ROSI. So... *(changing the subject)* ...what are you supposed to come and talk to me about?

HOMERO. Ah, yes - that. I've been looking for a job, but there's nothing out there!

ROSI. Nothing?

HOMERO. Well, nothing for someone like me...

ROSI. Someone like what?

HOMERO. ...someone who didn't even graduate from elementary school. I'm lucky I can read and write.

ROSI. Wanna know something?

HOMERO. Yeah?

ROSI. They're coming to look for you this very moment!

HOMERO. Who? For what?

ROSI. Well, you said you needed a job. So, it's for a job!

HOMERO. What kind of job? *¿Qué clase de trabajo?*

ROSI. Why do you ask so many questions? *¿No me crees?*

HOMERO. *¡Sí te creo!* Wait a minute! You say they're coming to look for me here? But I don't live here, so how do they know I'm here?

SIMÓN. *(Finishes eating and gets up from the table.)* I'm going to take a siesta. *¡Y no hablen muy fuerte!* (Grabs a cane.) Young kids nowadays. They think they can just yell all the time.

ROSI. I'll wake you in an hour, *papi. ¡Lo veo en una hora!*

(There is a knock at the door.)

ROSI. *(Once again grabs the knife.)* *¿Quién es?* Who is it?

MAN. *(Offstage)* I'm looking for... Homero.

HOMERO. *(Shocked)* How did you...?

ROSI. *¡Un momento por favor!* (Signals HOMERO to go to the door.)

HOMERO. *(Opens the door and walks outside.)* *¡Buenas! ¿Qué tal? Yo soy Homero.*

(They shake hands.)

ACT II

SCENE 3

Moments Later

HOMERO. *(Offstage)* Rosi, Rosi! Can you open up? *¡Rosi! ¿Me puedes abrir, por favor?*

ROSI. *(Cleans her hands from washing dishes. Opens the door.)* Did you forget to knock? *¿Ya no sabes tocar?*

HOMERO. *(Animated) Sí sé tocar. ¿Qué quieres que te toque? (Strums an imaginary guitar.) ¿Las mañanitas?* A serenade?

ROSI. You're a funny man now, eh? *¡Chistoso!*

HOMERO. I'm sorry, but I didn't want to wake up your father. Didn't he just tell us to keep it down? Or was it another elderly man who lives here?

ROSI. (Smiles) So, tell me, how did it go? *¿Te buscaban a tí?*

HOMERO. (Hugs her.) *¡Sí, gracias!* Thank you, thank you!

ROSI. *(Embarrassed from the hug.)* Do you or don't you have a job now?

HOMERO. *(Briefly holds her hand and looks into her eyes.)* I do. *(Beat)* I mean, I have a job! *¡Tengo chamba!*

ROSI. *¿Y qué clase de trabajo es?* What are you gonna be doing?

HOMERO. It's a loan company. They lend money! I've always said, 'If you wanna make money, go where the money is.' *Se necesita lana para hacer lana.*

ROSI. *(Laughs)* That's funny, 'cause that's also what bank robbers say!

HOMERO. Oh, now you're the comedian!

ROSI. I'm very happy for you, Homero. That's really good!

HOMERO. There's only a few, minor details...

ROSI. Oh?

HOMERO. Actually, there are three little problems...

ROSI. First it's details, now it's problems? Can you make up your mind? And why do you need to share these details, slash, problems with me? You know, it's very interesting how many things usually come in threes.

HOMERO. *(Distracted)* I'm sorry? I didn't hear you. Did you say, 'Good things don't grow on trees?'

ROSI. No, silly! I was talking about the number three. That good things, and bad, come in groups of threes!

HOMERO. *(Nervous laughter.)* Okay, let me tell you the first one.

ROSI. Wait. First, I need to sit down. *Esto se puede poner bueno. (Gestures to HOMERO to sit.)* Wanna sit?

HOMERO. No, I'm fine standing.

ROSI. Okay, shoot. *Dispara.*

HOMERO. First of all... the job is in the United States.

ROSI. Well, that's great! And just how is that a detail, slash, problem? *¡Yo no veo nada malo con eso!*

HOMERO. The problem is... that I would have to move there...

ROSI. And?

HOMERO. ... and my English is not very good.

ROSI. That's not a problem! There are many cities in the United States where there are more *Mejicanos* and other Spanish-speakers that you're gonna think you're still in *Méjico. (Taps herself on the shoulder.)* That was easy. Next detail, slash, problem.

HOMERO. Number two. The position is that of a collector.

ROSI. You mean, <u>you're</u> the one collecting the money?

HOMERO. Yes.

ROSI. *(Smiles)* Well, I don't see anything wrong with knocking on people's doors and asking for money. Do you? It's not like you're gonna have to break some knees, right?

HOMERO. No. You kidding? *(Rubs one of his knees.)* That hurts just thinking about it. But that's not the problem. The problem is... how am I going to *get* to these people's houses to ask for the money?

ROSI. You don't... *(Handles imaginary steering wheel.)* ... have a car?

HOMERO. *No. No tengo, pero ¡sí sé manejar!* I know how to drive!

ROSI. Okay, you can always borrow one, or rent it from a friend. *(Beat)* And the last thing, slash, something else?

HOMERO. Well, that's where Lupito comes in.

ROSI. What does he have to do with this? Is he in some sort of trouble?

HOMERO. No, nothing like that. I just needed to swing something by him.

ROSI. Since he's not here right now, you wanna "swing" it by me?

HOMERO. Well... it's a matter of... *(Nervous)...* of the heart.

ROSI. What's the matter? You have a weak heart? Do you need an operation? *(Points at him.)* That's it! You need an operation and you want my brother to donate his heart to you! *(Claps)* There, got it!

HOMERO. Don't make fun of me, Rosi. And besides, I've never heard of someone's heart being donated to someone else. I don't think it's humanly possible! So, I don't know where you get your information, but I think on this one you're way off. *(Laughs)* Imagine, putting someone's heart into someone else! Next thing you're gonna say is that you can make a brand new person from someone's kidney or liver!

ROSI. Well, maybe <u>that</u> technology doesn't exist yet, but I'd like to inform you of something, my dear expert-on-matters-of-the-heart.

HOMERO. What?

ROSI. Many women donate their hearts to other people all the time. Not only their hearts, but also their entire lives, their hard work, their loyalty, ...

HOMERO. I get it, I get it!

ROSI. Okay, so you want to wait for Lupito to get home from work so you can tell him your heart problem, right?

HOMERO. I don't know.

ROSI. How can you not know? What kind of man is that? *¡Alguien que no sabe!*

HOMERO. The kind that would be honored to go out with you. *(Proud of himself.)*

ROSI. *(Does a double take.)* Woah! Hold your horses... *(Closes her eyes and takes a deep breath.)* Did you just... ask me out?

HOMERO. Yes.

ROSI. On a date?

HOMERO. That's right.

ROSI. But, we don't know each other.

HOMERO. Yes we do. We met fourteen years ago. I'm Homero and you're Rosi!

ROSI. Great! What am I going to tell my father? *Papi,* I wanna go out with the spit champion? *¡No tiene trabajo, pero se avienta para escupir!* Doesn't have a job, but boy, is he good with phlegm!

HOMERO. I thought you were going to react like this. That's why I wanted to talk with Lupito first. Then, I thought he would back me up when I talked to your father.

ROSI. My father? Don't you think you're going a little <u>fast</u>? It's not a race, you know? Last I heard, women were the ones with the biological clock, not men. *(Throws her arms up in the air.)* Hey, but call me crazy! *Digan que soy loca. (Beat)* No, not me. You! *¡Tú! (Points at him.)¡Tú estás bien loco, Homero!*

HOMERO. *(Sings) ¡La verdad sí estoy loco, pero loco por ti!*

ROSI. Wow! And he sings too! What a combination - great spitter and great singer! But no job, no car, and no English. Minor <u>details</u>, he says. *(Beat)* Nope! I don't think it's gonna work! Nope!

Act II

SCENE 4

SETTING: *The Hacienda Grounds,*
Three Months Later
The grounds are decorated with red roses everywhere. There is live music playing and the celebration is in full force, with many couples dancing. A portable wooden dance floor is set up and may accommodate up to forty couples at any given moment. People constantly come to congratulate the newlyweds, HOMERO and ROSI. It is a beautiful evening and the stars are out.

HOMERO and ROSI have just finished their first meal together as husband and wife. They are now working on the wedding cake. ROSI looks stunning in a traditional, white wedding dress with fine, hand-made embroidery, which she learned from her mother, BETHZABÉ. HOMERO is wearing a black tuxedo with penguin tails. Solid colors look good on him. They're a handsome couple.

ROSI. Nope! I don't think it's gonna work! Nope!

HOMERO. Sure it is, honey! Look, let's ask your brother, Simoncito. He knows about these things. *(Spots SIMONCITO on the dance floor and waves at him.)* Simoncito! Over here! *Vente un ratito,¿sí?*

SIMONCITO. *(Hands off his dance partner to LUPITO and goes to the newlyweds.)* What's going on, you two? Are you having fun yet?

ROSI. We're having a blast, *hermano!* And also, I've never eaten as much as tonight. I'm afraid I may not be able to move tomorrow. Instead, I'll probably just roll everywhere I need to go. *(They laugh.)*

HOMERO. My wife is such a funny woman! And what timing! *(ROSI elbows HOMERO.)* Okay, okay. We'll ask you our question, Simoncito. Can you help us clear a little dilemma we have?

ROSI. We? I'm sorry, *esposo mio,* but I don't have a dilemma. It's you who has this dilemma. But go on... *(Smiles)*

HOMERO. Anyway, can you help us?

SIMONCITO. Sure, I'll try my best. Anything for my baby sister and my new *cuñado.*

HOMERO. Rosi says the car I've borrowed for my new job won't run with a motorcycle battery that I just came across. I say it will. And being that you're the expert with motor vehicles and all, what do you say?

SIMONCITO. That's your dilemma question?

ROSI. Yes.

SIMONCITO. I thought it was something... important. *(Sees a pretty lady walk by.)* Speaking of important... *(Starts to walk after her.)* ... I'll tell you after this dance.

HOMERO. *Mi amor,* why don't we forget about the battery for a little bit and see how good these shoes can move to the music, eh? *(Offers his arm.)* ¿*Bailamos?* Shall we dance?

ROSI. ¡*Seguro, mi esposo!* I thought you'd never ask!

(They dance.)

Act II

SCENE 5

SETTING: *SIMÓN FERNÁNDEZ Homestead,*
Five Years Later
Things are about the same, except that SIMÓN, who still gets around with his cane, now lives alone. However, he gets frequent visits from his children, who come with their respective children.

On this particular January day, HOMERO and ROSI come by to visit. They have brought their two girls to see their grandfather, who absolutely adores them. ROSI is pregnant at full term and, like in her two previous pregnancies, she glows. They enter the kitchen after having dropped off their luggage in the bedroom.

HOMERO. *¡Qué bonito venirlo a visitar, suegro!* It's so nice to visit you, *suegro.*

SIMÓN. As long as you bring my grand-daughters, I'm happy. *(Sees the grandkids and smiles. Opens his arms.)* Come here! Come here you two!

CHILDREN. Grandpa! Grandpa! *(They run to him.)*

SIMÓN. *(Turns to ROSI.) Mi'ja,* I'm so glad I got me these hearing aids now! Otherwise, how could I ever hear those beautiful bird songs calling out my name? *(Imitates a child's voice.)* Grandpa! Grandpa!

ROSI. *(Waddles and sits in a kitchen chair.)* What, *papi?*

SIMÓN. *(Laughs)* You wanna borrow one of them? *(Motions as if to remove one of his hearing aids.)*

ROSI. No, thanks. *(Turns to HOMERO.) Viejo,* I think we may be close to having number three right here! *(Points to the kitchen.)*

HOMERO. Are you okay? Oh, my God! *(Touches her forehead, then his, then her belly.)* I wasn't aware, *mi amor!* What do I do?

ROSI. First, relax and take your own pulse. They say that if you can't control yourself, how on earth are you supposed to control anything else?

HOMERO. Yes, yes! You're right! *(Does light pacing.)* You're always right!

ROSI. Okay, and second, I'm sure you were <u>aware</u>! Haven't you seen my big belly all these months? Hey, you were part of it!

HOMERO. *(Smiles)* I guess you're right, again. *(Beat)* Well, I was thinking that the best thing for the kids is if they're born in the United States, *mi amor.* After all, we want a better life for them, right?

ROSI. I hear you. But I also hear... *(Gets a contraction.)* ... and feel, this little one. And I think what he's trying to tell me is that he's gonna be a Mexican citizen, *viejo. (Gets another contraction and reacts to it.)*

SIMÓN. *(Calmly, while continuing to play with grandkids.)* You want me to call Dr. Ramón?

ROSI. Dr. Ramón, is he still around?

SIMÓN. Sure! But it's his son, Dr. Ramón Junior.

HOMERO. Is he any good? *(SIMÓN stares at HOMERO.)* I mean, does he have good bedside manners?

SIMÓN. *¡Yo no sé nada de* "manners"*!* All I know is that I think he's just as good as his father. *(Looks at ROSI.)* Well, <u>nobody</u> will ever compare to what the old Dr. Ramón did for my Rosi. Remember, *mi'ja?*

ROSI. How can I forget? It was a different kind of <u>fasting</u> program. Hey, but weight loss was essentially guaranteed. We should patent that bug and sell it. We'd be rich!

HOMERO. Hey, I'm all for rich. *(Beat)* Rosi, wasn't that illness caused by a tick? I vaguely remember the newspapers saying something to that effect.

ROSI. Yes, it was the typhoid fever. Nearly killed me.

SIMÓN. Homero, did you know that close to one-hundred people died from that thing in this area alone? It was an "epidemic." Hey, I finally got that word right!

HOMERO. I don't even know how to say it, *suegro.* Epi-ne-mic?

ROSI. Epi-... *(Gets a contraction.)* Never mind.

HOMERO. Was that when you saw your mother, *amor?* In your dream?

ROSI. It wasn't a dream, Homero. It was really her!

HOMERO. Oh, yes, yes. Sorry.

ROSI. *(Lightly cries.) Ese tiempo siempre me trae lágrimas.* I always get teary-eyed when I reminisce about those three, long weeks.

SIMÓN. Rosi, your mother would always remember what my *suegra* would predict about you, before you were even born.

ROSI. Yes, *papi.* Grandma was a special lady. She's the one that started our tradition.

SIMÓN. That's right! And now, that you yourself are a mother, do you have the same kinds of visions?

ROSI. You know, *papi,* I think my visions are getting stronger all the time. I don't know if it's my pregnancy hormones, or what.

HOMERO. Trust me, *suegro,* those hormones can be pretty powerful stuff!

ROSI. And *mamá* predicted something for me that is due right about now.

HOMERO. What was it? What did she say?

ROSI. She told me that my number three child would continue our special ways. She called him *Pepe Luis,* after the great torero.

HOMERO. I didn't even know that a bullfighter would <u>want</u> a name like "Pepe Luis."

ROSI. Well, this one did. Anyway, *mamá* said that my job in this world would not be finished until my number three was at least three years old.

SIMÓN. *Sí, mi'ja.* I remember her saying something like that. But don't think that you're gonna shoot for this baby to be three and then you're gonna hang up your gloves! No, ma'am! You're a fighter -- always were, always will be.

ROSI. *Sí, papi.* I hear you. *(Stronger contractions.)* Excuse me *papi.* Excuse me honey. I need to get up and move around. *(Stands)* I'll be back in a few minutes. Girls, listen to your father! *¡Y no se porten mal! (Exits)*

CHILDREN. Yes, *mamá!*

SIMÓN. *(Proud of his grandkids.)* Listen to that music! *(Turns to HOMERO.)* And if I want to lower the volume. For example, if I want to shut out the world, I simply turn this little knob... *(Turns it.)...* and ta-da! You don't have to hear anything you don't want to! Marvels of modern medicine. *Lo que es la ciencia!*

HOMERO. *Suegro*, can you give me the number to the Doctor?

SIMÓN. *(Plays with grandkids.)* ¡Esa es mi niétecita!

HOMERO. *(Louder)* ¡Suegro! Can you hear me? *(Stands in front of SIMON and waves.)*

SIMÓN. What? Oh, I forgot to turn these things up! *(Laughs and fixes hearing aids.)*

HOMERO. I was saying, can you give me the Doctor's number?

SIMÓN. Sure. It's inside that drawer there. *(Points to a drawer.)*

HOMERO. *(Opens the drawer and retrieves the number.)* Is this it? *(Shows it to SIMON.)*

SIMÓN. Yes, that's it!

HOMERO. *(Gets the phone and dials.)* Doctor Ramón? Yes, this is Homero, Rosi's husband. *(Beat)* Homero? *Sí*, Rosi Milagros' husband. Listen, my wife is going into labor right now. Can you come right away? *(Beat)* Okay. How long will it take you? *(Beat)* Ten minutes? Perfect! Hurry, Doctor, hurry! Thank you. We'll see you here.

SIMÓN. He says ten minutes; he'll be here in eight. That's the way his father was -- that's the way he is. Runs in the family.

(ROSI waddles back in.)

ROSI. Boy, this one's sure kicking a lot! Maybe he'll be a good soccer player or a karate kid?

CHILDREN. Soccer! Soccer! We want to play soccer! *(They jump up and down.)*

SIMÓN. I'm in heaven with my grandkids. They're like a little symphony. *(Looks up.)* Now, all I need is to be next to my Bethzabé. I'll go find you soon, *vieja. No te preocupes.* Don't you worry. *(He suddenly grabs his chest and writhes in pain.)*

HOMERO. *¡Suegro! ¿Qué le pasa?* Are you alright?

SIMÓN. Don't worry, Homero. It's just a damn elephant sitting on my chest. *(Catches his breath.)* Nothing a good elephant rifle can't take care of.

(SIMON and ROSI start getting their pains synchronized.)

ROSI. *Papi,* are... you... okay?

SIMÓN. *Mi'ja,* are... *you...* okay?

HOMERO. *(Looks at one, then the other.)* What do I do? What do I do? *(Looks at the kids, and picks them up. (A rapid knock on the door is heard.)*

ROSI. There's the doctor, Homero! Let him in!

SIMÓN. Huh? What's that? Bethzabé? Is that you?

HOMERO. *(Runs to the door. Puts the girls down.)* Doctor? Come in, hurry!

(DR. RAMÓN JUNIOR enters.)

DR. RAMÓN JUNIOR. *(Goes to ROSI.)* How close together are your contractions?

ROSI. Don't worry about me, Doctor! Go with my father! He's having a heart attack! I'll be... *(Gets a contraction.)*... okay!

DR. RAMÓN JUNIOR. *(Turns and sees SIMÓN crouched over the table.)* Don Simón, Don Simón! Can you hear me?

SIMÓN. Yes, Bethzabé, I can hear you!

DR. RAMÓN JUNIOR. I'm Doctor Ramón Junior. *(Takes out a pen light and examines SIMÓN'S eyes.)* Where's your pain?

SIMÓN. I love you, *mi vieja!* I saw the light already! I'll be right there! *(He collapses.)*

DR. RAMÓN JUNIOR. *(Initiates CPR.)* C'mon, Don Simón, you can make it! You can make it! Don't give up! *(Looks at HOMERO.)* Bring me some wet towels, hurry!

(HOMERO goes off for the towels, taking the kids with him.)

ROSI. ¡Adiós, papi, adiós! ¡Te quiero mucho! ¡Saludas a mamá! *(Gets a strong contraction and yells.)* Ahhhh!

DR. RAMÓN JUNIOR. *(Turns to ROSI.)* Are you okay?

ROSI. Come here, doctor! I'm ready. You can leave my father now. He wants to be with my mother. *(Yells)* My baby and I need you!

(DR. RAMÓN JUNIOR obliges.)

DR. RAMÓN JUNIOR. *(Puts on some gloves and examines ROSI.)* The baby's already there! He's crowning! Push, Rosi, push!

(ROSI pushes once and the baby is delivered.)

DR. RAMÓN JUNIOR. *(Attends the newborn.)* There you go! Come and say hi to your mother!

(Newborn crying is heard. ROSI also cries. HOMERO enters with the GIRLS.)

HOMERO. Oh, it's a boy! Our Pepe Luis! Congratulations, *vieja!* You did it *(Hugs and kisses ROSI.)*

ROSI. Homero, please go to my father and lay him on his bed. He's resting now.

(HOMERO does as he's told.)

DR. RAMÓN JUNIOR. You're a very brave woman, Rosi.

ROSI. Doctor, my mother once told me that sometimes a life has to be lost in order to save another. Right now, I believe my father saved my baby, Pepe Luis.

DR. RAMÓN JUNIOR. *Usted es un verdadero milagro, Rosi.* I don't know how you do it! But I believe you are one of God's miracles!

(The baby cries a healthy cry.)

ROSI. That's it, *mi'jo!* Exercise those baby lungs of yours! That's it!

CHILDREN. *(Singing a symphony.)* ¡Rosi Milagros! ¡Rosi Milagros!

THE END

GRAND CHAMPION
Special Edition Cards
2016

8th Dan Tae Kwon Do

Jay-el HINOJOSA, MD

ABOUT THE AUTHOR

José Luis "Jay-el" Hinojosa, MD and his family emigrated from Mexico to the USA when he was only 7 years old. He was fortunate to attend an Ivy League school (Brown University) for his undergraduate studies, after which he matriculated at the University of Cincinnati College of Medicine (Cincinnati, OH) to earn his Doctor of Medicine degree. After completing his specialty in Family Medicine in south Texas, he had a successful private practice for 25 years.

Today, he is Chief of Staff at Stanton County Hospital and Medical Director at Stanton County Family Practice in Johnson, Kansas. Always wanting to continue learning, he will attain his Masters of Science in Healthcare Administration from Grand Canyon University in early 2016.

Besides being a physician leader, Dr. Hinojosa is also a martial arts leader. He has trained and taught the martial arts for 40 years and has won many titles, including *World Championships* in Germany and México, multiple Hall of Fame awards, including a *Lifetime Achievement Award*, and he is a crowd favorite with his powerful, creative, and highly entertaining routines – most notably, his award winning form entitled *Reflections of an Old Man*, where he dresses up as an elderly man with a cane and dazzles the crowd while reminiscing about his youth. Speaking of youth, Dr. Hinojosa has three children (JL, Laura, and Alexis) who always inspire him; he is also happily married to Maria Elena Hinojosa.

As an innovator, Dr. Hinojosa invented a fascinating medical device (patent pending) that is positioned to revolutionize health care around the globe – please go to www.TheMDMedical.com for more information on this. He also invented the popular game *Grand Champion®,* the first ever card game related to the martial arts and it teaches good moral values.

This second edition of *Rosi Milagros* marks the 12th book authored by Dr. Hinojosa and his first play. *Rosi Milagros* was inspired by true events... and true individuals. Simón and Bethzabé Fernández were Dr. Hinojosa's maternal grandparents; Rosi and Homero Hinojosa were his parents; and he was known as *Pepe Luis* when he was young.

Dr. Hinojosa co-wrote the screenplay for an independent feature length film (*Campeón: A Journey of the Heart*). He just finished penning his first book entirely (yes, 100%) in Spanish, entitled *¡El Lenguaje de los Triunfadores!* It is the Spanish version of his highly-popular personal improvement book, *The Language of Winners!* He is currently working on the Spanish version of *Master and Disciple* and cannot wait to release it to his Spanish-speaking family, friends, and followers. For more information on how to get ahold of any of his books, please go to www.BooksByDrHinojosa.com

Dr. Hinojosa is a stage actor and has also appeared in several feature-length films. His most recent acting work was in the world premiere run (Nov. 2011 and Jan. 2012 in three south Texas cities) of *Tales of the Hidalgo Pump House*, where he played one of the lead characters, Luis Rivera, and had the opportunity to display his singing, dancing, and comedic timing; in his most recent film, he played the villain in the feature-length 2009 Warrior Pictures film *Campeón: A Journey of the Heart.*

As a professional speaker, Dr. Hinojosa is equally fluent in Spanish as he is in English keynote presentations. He shares his experiences with his audiences with such passion and clarity, that he always "connects." It is no wonder that Dr. José Luis "Jay-el" Hinojosa is highly sought out as a motivational and inspirational speaker not only in the USA, but also in México. He is a specialist in *Leadership and Success* topics, with his most popular keynotes being: *The Making of a Leader, Dream Your Way to Success, The Five Business Lessons to Learn from Breaking Boards, and Develop a World Champion Attitude.*

DID YOU ENJOY THIS BOOK?

- Students, did this book inspire you to want to see it as a live production on stage?

- Teachers, do you think you'd like to produce *Rosi Milagros* at your school or in your community? If so, just send me an e-mail at DrH@TheMDMedical.com and we can make it happen!

- Would you recommend this book to your friends and loved ones?

If so, show the world that you care and order a copy of *Rosi Milagros* for your friends and loved ones right now!

HERE'S HOW TO ORDER

www.BooksByDrHinojosa.com

The cover of the first edition of *Rosi Milagros* features a portrait of my mother, Rosalinda "Rosi" Fernández de Hinojosa.

www.ingramcontent.com/pod-product-compliance
Lightning Source LLC
LaVergne TN
LVHW091204080426
835509LV00006B/823